Springer Texts in Education

Springer Texts in Education delivers high-quality instructional content for graduates and advanced graduates in all areas of Education and Educational Research. The textbook series is comprised of self-contained books with a broad and comprehensive coverage that are suitable for class as well as for individual self-study. All texts are authored by established experts in their fields and offer a solid methodological background, accompanied by pedagogical materials to serve students such as practical examples, exercises, case studies etc. Textbooks published in the Springer Texts in Education series are addressed to graduate and advanced graduate students, but also to researchers as important resources for their education, knowledge and teaching. Please contact Yoka Janssen at Yoka.Janssen@springer.com or your regular editorial contact person for queries or to submit your book proposal.

Irina Lyublinskaya · Xiaoxue Du

A Pedagogical Framework for K–12 AI Literacy

Development, Validation, and Applications in Teacher Education

Springer

Irina Lyublinskaya
Teachers College
Columbia University
New York, NY, USA

Xiaoxue Du
Bill and Melinda Gates Foundation
Seattle, WA, USA

ISSN 2366-7672 ISSN 2366-7680 (electronic)
Springer Texts in Education
ISBN 978-3-032-23569-5 ISBN 978-3-032-23570-1 (eBook)
https://doi.org/10.1007/978-3-032-23570-1

This Springer imprint is published by the registered company Springer Nature Switzerland AG
The registered company address is: Gewerbestrasse 11, 6330 Cham, Switzerland

Preface

Artificial Intelligence (AI) is no longer a distant promise—it is a defining force of our time, reshaping how people learn, work, and interact. For education, this transformation brings both a profound challenge and a possibility. Around the world, educators are being asked not only to use AI tools but to help students understand, critique, and shape the systems that increasingly govern social and civic life. Yet, despite growing attention to AI in schools, most efforts remain fragmented, often emphasizing tools over understanding, or access over agency.

We wrote this book because we believe AI literacy must become a cornerstone of twenty-first-century education—anchored not in technical fluency alone, but in ethical reflection, civic responsibility, and human development. Our work emerged from a shared conviction that students deserve to engage with AI not merely as consumers but as co-creators and critical thinkers. We saw a clear gap: while numerous theoretical frameworks define what AI literacy is, few provide a cohesive, evidence-based model for translating these ideas into scalable pedagogical practice.

This book is a response to that gap. It is a work of applied educational research that explicitly bridges the conceptual and the empirical. We first move beyond abstract debates to offer a rigorously developed and validated pedagogical framework for AI literacy (Theory), and then proceed to demonstrate and evaluate its application in teacher preparation (Practice). Crucially, the book presents, for the first time, a cross-national empirical study comparing how preservice teachers in two global powers—the United States and China—develop the competencies, ethical reasoning, and instructional confidence needed to implement AI literacy responsibly.

Our intended audience is broad but united by purpose: educators seeking practical guidance; policymakers shaping digital and AI education strategies; and researchers advancing the global conversation on responsible AI, equity, and learning. We situate this work within current debates on digital citizenship and the future of work domains where education systems must act decisively to ensure that AI serves human flourishing rather than deepening inequities.

This project has been a journey of collaboration and reflection. It began as a question shared among colleagues and students: *What would it take to teach AI meaningfully, not just use it?* From that question grew years of curriculum design, teacher partnerships, and comparative research. Along the way, we encountered the same technologies we were studying—large language models, adaptive systems, and automated analytics—which shaped both our thinking and our methods. We acknowledge that this book itself was informed by the responsible use of Generative AI (GenAI) tools for drafting, synthesis, and analysis, always guided by human judgment and scholarly rigor.

Above all, this work is grounded in hope—the hope that teachers and learners everywhere can engage with AI as a space for creativity, inquiry, and shared humanity. We invite readers to join us in reimagining what education can become in an age when intelligence, both human and artificial, is deeply intertwined.

New York, USA Irina Lyublinskaya
Seattle, USA Xiaoxue Du

Contents

About the Authors

Dr. Irina Lyublinskaya is a Professor of Mathematics and Education at Teachers College, Columbia University, New York. She holds Ph.D. in Theoretical and Mathematical Physics from the Leningrad State University, Russia. She taught high school and university mathematics and science for 40 years. She is a recipient of various awards, including Radioshack/Tandy Prize for Teaching Excellence in Mathematics, Science, and Computer Science, NSTA Distinguished Science Teaching Award and citation, Education's Unsung Heroes Award for innovation in the classroom, and NSTA Vernier Technology Award. Her research interests are in the areas of AI literacy, STEM education, teacher education, curriculum development, and international comparative education. She authored/co-authored 23 books, 16 book chapters, and over 100 peer-reviewed papers and proceedings in these fields.

Dr. Xiaoxue Du is the Senior Program Officer for AI Innovation & Access at the Bill & Melinda Gates Foundation. Her background includes work with a leading consulting firm on AI-enabled product strategy and digital transformation, as well as research and teaching experience at the MIT Media Lab focused on AI literacy and human–AI interaction. Dr. Du's academic work centers on helping learners and educators understand and responsibly engage with emerging AI systems. She earned her doctorate from Teachers College, Columbia University, where she used mixed-methods approaches to study complex sociotechnical systems.

Part I
AI in Education and AI Education

This part of the book provides the theoretical and conceptual foundation for our study, establishing the urgent need for integrating AI literacy into K–12 education. Our objective in this part is twofold: to frame the profound impact of Artificial Intelligence on the learning ecosystem and to identify the specific conceptual gaps that necessitate the novel pedagogical framework developed in Part II.

First, Chap. 1 offers a systematic review and critical synthesis of AI's rapid expansion within educational settings. This chapter examines both the transformative potential and the emerging challenges of AI integration, providing a balanced view of how intelligent systems can enhance personalized learning, streamline administrative processes, and enrich instructional design. Concurrently, it addresses critical issues related to privacy, algorithmic bias, and equitable access. The chapter concludes with a pivotal argument: in an era increasingly shaped by intelligent systems, AI literacy represents a foundational, rather than specialized, competency for all members of the educational ecosystem.

Chapter 2 then explores the evolving global landscape of AI literacy frameworks and curricula. This comprehensive review maps the conceptual terrain of AI literacy by identifying shared principles, recurring themes, and, crucially, the persistent gaps in current approaches. It highlights a growing consensus on the multidimensional nature of AI literacy—combining technical understanding, ethical evaluation, and responsible use—but underscores the absence of actionable pedagogical models that effectively translate these principles for classroom teachers.

Together, these two chapters define the educational rationale for AI literacy, clarify its complex scope, and establish the urgent, unmet need for a validated, practice-oriented design. They successfully lay the groundwork for the framework development and empirical validation studies presented in Part II.

Chapter 1
Opportunities and Challenges of AI Use in Education

Abstract This chapter synthesizes existing research on the opportunities and challenges of Artificial Intelligence (AI) use in K-12 education. AI technologies offer significant promise, including the potential to transform learning environments. Opportunities explored in this review include how AI can personalize learning by adapting to individual student needs and thought processes, support teacher decision-making with real-time, data-driven insights that free up time for higher-order instruction, and foster student skills in creativity, metacognition, and ethical reflection by positioning AI as a critical partner in inquiry. However, the rapid adoption of AI also raises critical concerns. Challenges examined include the threat of algorithmic bias, privacy risks, and surveillance in educational settings, which can undermine trust and reinforce inequities. The review also highlights significant gaps in teacher professional development and AI readiness. Finally, it addresses the risk of over-reliance on automation, which can lead to the 'deskilling' of educators and a reduction in students' critical thinking abilities if AI is not implemented thoughtfully. The chapter concludes by arguing that AI literacy is an essential foundational competency for civic participation, workforce equity, and educational justice in the modern era.

1.1 Introduction

Artificial Intelligence (AI) is transforming the foundations of modern society—reshaping the workforce, reconfiguring civic engagement, and revolutionizing how knowledge is created, distributed, and applied (Bentley, 2025). From predictive algorithms used in hiring and healthcare to generative models that produce texts, images, and codes, AI technologies are increasingly embedded in daily life. Tools such as recommendation systems, virtual assistants, facial recognition software, and large language models are changing how we access information and how decisions are made—often invisibly and at scale, guided by algorithms that operate behind the scenes. Specifically, as AI becomes more pervasive, concerns about privacy, bias, and surveillance are emerging as critical ethical challenges. These concerns extend beyond technical design—they shape how individuals and institutions perceive and

I. Lyublinskaya and X. Du, *A Pedagogical Framework for K–12 AI Literacy*, Springer Texts in Education, https://doi.org/10.1007/978-3-032-23570-1_1

adopt AI. Individuals' willingness to use AI tools has been found to depend on their trust in data protection, fairness, and transparency measures (Viberg et al., 2025). When privacy is uncertain or algorithmic decisions seem opaque, even well-intentioned AI innovations risk being met with resistance (Holmes & Porayska-Pomsta, 2023). This tension between promise and precaution reflects a broader societal challenge: ensuring that AI systems, while powerful, remain accountable, human-centered, and aligned with the values of those they serve (Cubio, 2025).

AI's transformative power is also reshaping the educational landscape (Cantú-Ortiz et al., 2020). From adaptive learning platforms that tailor content to individual students to intelligent tutoring systems that provide personalized feedback, the integration of AI holds great promise for revolutionizing how we teach and learn. However, the rapid adoption of these technologies also raises critical questions (Owoc et al., 2021). This chapter synthesizes existing research on the opportunities and challenges of AI use in education. It highlights how AI can personalize learning, support teacher decision-making, and expand access for marginalized students. At the same time, it examines challenges of AI use around bias, privacy, misinformation as well as the risk of over-reliance on automation leading to reduction in teacher's professional autonomy and creative input and a decline in students' critical thinking and problem-solving abilities. The chapter concludes with the argument that AI literacy is an essential digital competency for civic participation, workforce equity, and educational justice in the era of AI.

1.2 Opportunities of AI in education

The integration of AI technologies into K-12 education offers significant opportunities to address long-standing challenges and create more dynamic learning environments. This section highlights how AI tools can be used to foster deeper student understanding by uncovering their reasoning, support teacher decision-making with data-driven insights, and promote equitable access to education for all students.

1.2.1 Support for Student Learning

AI technologies are reshaping how students learn by enabling more personalized, inclusive, and creative educational experiences (Zha et al., 2024). Instead of delivering one-size-fits-all lessons, teachers can implement AI systems that adapt in real time to individual student's needs by analyzing their thought process, identifying areas of struggle, and providing tailored support to help them advance (Halkiopoulos & Gkintoni, 2024). Tan et al. (2025) demonstrated how AI-driven platforms can detect patterns in students' problem-solving, identify specific conceptual misunderstandings, and suggest next-step feedback tailored to each learner. Their systematic review revealed that such adaptive systems, ranging from intelligent tutoring programs to AI-enabled learning analytics, allow educators to move beyond uniform instruction toward more responsive, data-informed teaching. AI-powered tools can automatically analyze learners' input in real time, diagnose where reasoning breaks down, and generate feedback aligned with the learner's individual progress. For instance, AI-assisted assessment platforms and conversational tutoring agents can provide nuanced feedback on students' written work, mathematical reasoning, or coding logic, supporting teachers in offering targeted interventions rather than broad explanations (Kalyani et al., 2025). Moreover, the literature analysis indicated that these systems enhance both formative assessment and teacher decision-making, enabling educators to focus on higher-order tasks such as designing creative inquiry experiences or facilitating conceptual transfer (Lee & Kwon, 2024).

Studies show that the use of AI systems is leading to a shift away from uniform pacing and standardized content delivery toward a more responsive, data-informed approach to teaching and learning (Panaoura, 2025). As Panaoura (2025) notes, such tools not only enhance procedural fluency but also foster metacognitive growth helping students recognize their own learning needs, monitor progress, and develop persistence in solving complex problems. For educators, such data-informed insights make it possible to design lessons that balance challenge and support, thereby promoting both equity and engagement in diverse classrooms (Li & Wilson, 2025). In this way, AI contributes to a broader pedagogical transformation: from static content delivery toward an iterative model of learning that values reflection, adaptation, and continuous improvement.

Research findings show that Generative AI (GenAI) tools can scaffold instruction across disciplines in ways that reduce cognitive load while preserving learner autonomy and creativity (Li & Wilson, 2025; Suryani et al., 2024). In writing instruction, Li and Wilson (2025) found that AI-integrated scaffolding can play a crucial role in supporting students' creative and metacognitive engagement in writing tasks. Their systematic review of K–12 classrooms identified three key functions of AI support: cognitive, creative, and linguistic. Cognitive support tools like grammar correction and idea organization systems help students manage cognitive load, freeing mental resources for higher-order thinking. When students engage with GenAI in these ways, they are prompted to evaluate outputs, question assumptions, and refine their thinking. Creative support systems, such as narrative generators or ideation assistants, encourage experimentation and risk-taking, positioning students as decision-makers who evaluate and adapt AI suggestions. Language enhancement tools aid vocabulary development and stylistic refinement, promoting confidence and expressive range (Li & Wilson, 2025).. In science classrooms, AI-based simulation tools such as LabTutor AI and intelligent virtual labs encourage students to question experimental assumptions, interpret unexpected results, and evaluate the quality of evidence (Kestin et al., 2025). Specifically, Kestin et al. (2025) demonstrated that such AI-powered tutoring systems allowed students to achieve significantly higher learning gains in less time compared to traditional active learning classes. This support stemmed from the tool's ability to provide personalized, on-demand feedback and allow for self-pacing, enabling learners to fill conceptual gaps without the pressure of synchronous classroom speed. Furthermore, students reported feeling more engaged and motivated, as the AI scaffolded complex problem-solving steps rather than simply providing answers. In mathematics, Awang et al. (2025) distinguish between pedagogical AI tools, which scaffold learning through adaptation, and GenAI tools, which offer step-by-step problem-solving support. Adaptive platforms (such as Squirrel AI) help learners recognize reasoning errors and test alternative strategies by dynamically adjusting task difficulty in real time.. AI-driven tools can analyze students' strengths, weaknesses, and cognitive patterns to create personalized learning trajectories, ensuring that every learner progresses at an appropriate pace. This adaptability allows instruction to move beyond the uniform teaching model by dynamically adjusting task difficulty, recommending targeted resources, and providing real-time feedback that addresses individual misconceptions. In creative writing and visual arts, generative tools like can scaffold student inquiry and expression while fostering agency. For instance, Ravi et al. (2025) showed that LLMs can assist students in drafting storylines, such as for a comic book analyzing literary tropes, provided learners retain control over revision and critique. This interaction supported students by creating space for them to test hypotheses, negotiate group decisions, and refine their artifacts through iterative feedback loops. Similarly, engaging with tools like Sudowrite or Stable Diffusion prompts deep reflection on ownership and authorship (Rafner et al., 2025). Rafner et al. (2025) found that students actively maintained their agency through specific strategies like "selective appropriation" (curating specific AI suggestions) or "counter-inspiration" (deliberately rejecting AI outputs to assert originality).. These moments of reflection foster deeper learning and help students develop critical awareness of how AI systems work and where they can go wrong.

Ultimately, the educational value of these technologies depends entirely on thoughtful teacher guidance. Li and Wilson (2025) emphasize that these benefits are realized only when educators design activities that balance guidance and independence, ensuring that AI serves as a "machine-in-the-loop" collaborator that extends student agency rather than replacing it. Research indicates that students are most engaged when teachers encourage them to treat AI as a "thinking partner" by questioning outputs and iteratively improving designs rather than accepting the first solution offered (Zha et al., 2024). When teachers guide these interactions thoughtfully, AI becomes not just a tool for learning, but a lens through which students examine ethical values embedded in technology (McStay & Rosner, 2021). Yet, realizing this potential depends on sustained teacher professional development (PD) and clear ethical frameworks to ensure that AI functions as a partner in learning by augmenting, not replacing, the human dimension of teaching.

1.2.2 Support for Teachers

AI technologies are reshaping not only student learning, but also how teachers plan, reflect, and make instructional decisions. Research demonstrates that these tools serve as first-draft accelerators: teachers report saving up to 31% of lesson-planning time—equating to several hours weekly (National Foundation for Educational Research,

2024) —which frees cognitive bandwidth for tasks like customizing instruction, strengthening student relationships, and engaging in higher-order design work. For instance, the *LessonPlanner* system improved novice teachers' planning quality while reducing workload (Fan et al., 2024). Developed through a formative co-design process with early-career educators, LessonPlanner combines large language model (LLM) generation with structured pedagogical scaffolds to support the development of coherent, evidence-based lesson plans. The system guides users through stages such as setting learning objectives, sequencing instructional events, and generating corresponding teaching materials, all aligned with Gagné's framework for effective instruction (Gagné et al., 1992). In controlled studies, participants who used Lesson-Planner produced lesson plans that were significantly higher in quality demonstrating better alignment of objectives, strategies, and assessments than those developed using standard ChatGPT interfaces. Expert interviews further confirmed that the structured outline and visible event cues helped educators conceptualize lessons more holistically and integrate both theoretical and practical components with greater confidence (Fan et al., 2024). Moreover, empirical studies indicate that the use of AI-enabled tools reduces teachers' mental and temporal demands and alleviates the cognitive load typically associated with iterative lesson design (Belloula, 2025). Thus, the pedagogy-driven AI design, which embeds educational theory directly into the generative workflow, offers a promising model for empowering teachers to focus on creativity, personalization, and student engagement while maintaining professional agency over instructional decisions.

Similarly, Ravi et al. (2025) emphasize that when teachers participate directly in shaping LLM-based project-based learning (PBL) tools, these systems better align with authentic classroom challenges such as balancing open-ended inquiry with curriculum standards, managing group dynamics, and providing ongoing formative feedback. Teachers in this study envisioned AI companions that could help scaffold brainstorming, generate differentiated rubrics, and visualize progress without automating core pedagogical judgment. By automating routine design and management tasks, LLMs can free teachers to focus on mentoring, while students gain space to test hypotheses, negotiate group decisions, and refine their artifacts through iterative feedback loops. Moreover, educators highlighted ethical and equity dimensions: tools must preserve transparency, avoid bias, and uphold student privacy while strengthening teachers' professional agency (Ravi et al., 2025). When these design principles are followed, GenAI can become an enabler of high-quality PBL helping teachers cultivate creativity, critical thinking, and reflection as students engage in meaningful, interdisciplinary projects that mirror real-world inquiry.

AI-enabled dashboards and learning analytics platforms provide a new layer of insights into student learning trends. Rather than relying solely on assessments or classroom observation, teachers can access real-time data on where students are struggling, which concepts are misunderstood, or who might be disengaged (Salas-Pilco et al., 2022). Unlike traditional data dashboards, AI-enhanced learning analytics systems apply machine-learning models to detect latent misconceptions and predict learning trajectories in real time. For example, Tan et al. (2025) describe how neural-network-based error-pattern analysis identified underlying conceptual gaps that would have been invisible through conventional item analysis. Teachers could then receive automated prompts suggesting targeted interventions at a level of granularity and adaptivity beyond earlier analytics approaches. Their systematic review highlights how advanced AI-driven diagnostic systems, particularly those leveraging deep learning architectures, can move beyond surface-level correctness scoring to capture students' reasoning trajectories and misconceptions. By analyzing patterns in student responses across large datasets, neural network models can detect latent knowledge structures, revealing, for example, whether a learner's repeated errors stem from procedural mistakes or deeper conceptual misunderstandings. In practical classroom use, teachers leverage these systems to create personalized learning tasks and individual education plans, enabling differentiated support such as conceptual reteaching for one group and enrichment challenges for another (Collie et al., 2024). Tan et al. (2025) emphasize that this capacity to interpret learning processes, not just outcomes, represents a paradigm shift in educational analytics: AI tools are no longer passive evaluators but active partners in formative assessment and instructional decision-making. However, the authors also caution that without appropriate teacher training and ethical guidelines, these technologies risk reinforcing data dependency and reducing teachers' interpretive agency (Holmes & Porayska-Pomsta, 2023), a reminder that pedagogical insights must remain central even as analytics grow increasingly intelligent.

In addition to the instructional support, AI has begun to shape new pathways for teacher PD. Much like adaptive platforms for students, intelligent systems can be used to personalize adult learning. Kumari et al. (2025) found that AI-driven tools, ranging from intelligent tutoring systems to virtual micro-teaching simulations, allow teachers to engage in risk-free practice and receive tailored resources based on their specific skill gaps. Their study reported that 83% of participants improved their instructional design competency through these adaptive platforms, which provided differentiated learning paths for novice versus advanced users. Beyond training modules, AI tools can analyze actual teaching practice to provide scalable mentorship. Demszky et al. (2023) demonstrated this with M-Powering Teachers, an NLP tool that analyzes classroom transcripts to provide feedback on how well teachers build on student ideas. In their randomized trial, teachers who reviewed this automated, non-judgmental feedback significantly increased their use of high-quality instructional strategies, such as asking follow-up questions, by 13%. While these tools focus on skill refinement, other models emphasize co-learning. Dai's (2025) study offers a robust model for teacher PD by situating AI learning within collaborative inquiry. By co-engaging with students in projects spanning from unplugged activities to digital creation teachers moved past viewing AI as a threat. Instead, reported that this co-engagement demystified the technology and enhanced their pedagogical confidence, allowing them to shape AI tools with intention (Dai, 2025). Ultimately, this model reframes AI learning as a participatory and relational endeavor where teachers and students co-construct understanding, directly enhancing the teacher's instructional agency in the age of intelligent technologies.

The potential of AI in education extends well beyond providing tools for content creation or analytics; it also cultivates teacher agency. Kalyani et al. (2025) found that pre-service teachers using AI-based assessment systems reported significant improvements in both reflective practice and self-efficacy, suggesting that these tools can serve as professional mirrors that provoke deeper self-analysis. Teachers exposed to AI-generated feedback often begin questioning which pedagogical decisions should remain human, how AI-suggested feedback might influence student identity, and what assumptions lie beneath algorithmic prompts. Viberg et al. (2025) also note that teachers with higher AI self-efficacy and understanding are more likely to trust and meaningfully engage with AI systems. Their study of K–12 teachers across six countries shows that confidence in AI competence predicts a more realistic appreciation of benefits and fewer concerns,, positioning teachers as informed evaluators rather than passive implementers. Teachers who perceive themselves as knowledgeable about AI are better equipped to question algorithmic outputs and contextualize AI-generated insights. Conversely, low confidence often results in resistance or dependence, underscoring the need for PD that fosters both technical understanding and reflective capacity. Furthermore, Collie et al. (2024) demonstrate that this agency is strongly linked to institutional context; their research indicates that when schools provide robust GenAI support, teachers report higher self-efficacy and valuing of the technology, which in turn drives them to actively integrate AI into their teaching and student learning activities.. Together, this body of research makes clear that when educators are prepared to interrogate, adapt, and align AI outputs with their values, AI becomes a catalyst for professional development rather than a replacement for human expertise.

1.3 Challenges of AI in education

While AI offers significant opportunities, its implementation also introduces a new set of complex challenges. This section examines the ethical and practical concerns surrounding the use of AI in K-12 education, including issues of privacy, algorithmic bias, infrastructural inequity, teacher readiness, and the risk of over-reliance on automation.

1.3.1 Privacy, Surveillance, and Algorithmic Injustice in AI-Powered Education

AI tools such as facial recognition, emotion-detection, keystroke logging, and webcam surveillance raise urgent ethical and pedagogical concerns in K–12 settings. These systems often collect sensitive data continuously—from academic responses to biometric and behavioral cues—without transparent consent or limits on how data are used or retained. Students, families, and even educators are frequently unaware of how such data is gathered, stored, or shared, deeply undermining trust and informed choice in educational environments. Such AI-based monitoring shifts classroom culture from collaboration to compliance, particularly in under-resourced schools where privacy protections are weaker and surveillance is more common (Andrejevic & Selwyn, 2020). As Andrejevic and Selwyn (2020) explain, the normalization of facial recognition and emotion-detection systems in schools extends long-standing surveillance practices into new algorithmic forms of control. These technologies promise safety and efficiency but instead risk institutionalizing a "mechanical gaze" that measures student engagement through facial expressions, attendance, and affective cues. In resource-limited contexts, where governance structures and data-protection protocols are often underdeveloped, such systems can entrench asymmetric power relations: students become continuously observable data subjects, while teachers are positioned as enforcers of algorithmic norms rather than facilitators of dialogue. The authors warn that facial recognition initiatives can reconfigure schools along authoritarian and exclusionary lines, reducing trust, marginalizing vulnerable groups, and eroding the pedagogical space for experimentation and error. By replacing human judgment with automated detection, AI surveillance narrows the social and emotional dimensions of learning, transforming the classroom into a site of compliance rather than creativity (Andrejevic & Selwyn, 2020).

Research shows that algorithmic surveillance erodes student autonomy and performance. While proponents like Salloum et al. (2025) demonstrate that AI models can now detect student emotions with 95% accuracy to theoretically enhance engagement, critical research suggests these systems may trigger negative behavioral responses Individuals subject to AI monitoring report lower perceived agency and higher resistance compared to human oversight often leading to poorer engagement and compliance motivation (Schlund & Zitek, 2024). For instance, Schlund and Zitek (2024) found that participants under automated or algorithmic observation exhibited lower perceived autonomy, increased criticism of the surveillance, and lower task persistence compared to those monitored by human instructors. These findings highlight a paradox in AI-mediated learning: systems designed to enhance responsiveness may, if implemented without care, constrain agency and undermine the very emotional and cognitive autonomy that education seeks to foster.

Teachers also voice deep concerns about algorithmic bias and the erosion of professional judgment. Röhl (2025) shows that algorithmic tools, while marketed as objective and efficient, often redistribute authority away from teachers and toward opaque technical infrastructures. Educators expressed frustration that the system's standardization processes failed to account for contextual judgment, challenging their professional autonomy. Teachers also reported anxiety about being compelled to justify deviations from automated outputs, a dynamic that Röhl (2025) argues transforms educators from trusted interpreters of learning into overseers of data-driven accountability systems.

Another concern is emotion-tracking tools, particularly in remote or hybrid learning contexts. These tools offer no proven benefit for academic safety or emotional support but introduce privacy risks. The deployment of tools like Gaggle or Securly has reportedly flagged sensitive content, with punitive outcomes such as undesired outing, misinterpretation, or unnecessary referrals to authorities. Systems operating under the guise of personalization or safety can instead reinforce structural inequities channeling marginalized students into pathways of discipline rather than enrichment. Without inclusive design processes, bias audits, or transparent data practices, AI may perpetuate inequitable outcomes in grading, behavioral alerts, and evaluation (Holmes & Porayska-Pomsta, 2023) Holmes and Porayska-Pomsta (2023) caution that emotion-sensing technologies frequently rely on narrow, non-representative datasets that misread difference as deviance, reinforcing deficit perspectives. When embedded in school systems, they shift the balance from care to control, eroding trust and reducing both teacher and student agency.

Finally, these ethical and infrastructural challenges are compounded by a lack of broader regulatory frameworks. The rapid pace of AI development has outstripped educational policy, leaving schools to navigate a "regulatory vacuum" regarding data ownership, liability, and age-appropriate design. Schiff (2022) attributes this gap to a prevalent policy imbalance: national AI strategies overwhelmingly prioritize "Education for AI", e.g., training a workforce to ensure economic competitiveness, while largely neglecting "AI for Education" and its ethical governance. Consequently, while policymakers focus on generating AI talent, the specific risks of deploying AI tools in schools receive scant attention, leaving the ethical implications of these technologies unregulated. Unlike established educational technologies governed by clear protocols, such as COPPA (Federal Trade Commission, n.d.) or FERPA (U.S. Department of Education, n.d.) in the United States, GenAI introduces gray areas regarding the ownership of student-generated prompts and the liability for AI-generated errors or harmful content. School leaders are often forced to make high-stakes procurement decisions without standardized safety benchmarks or clear federal guidance. This regulatory lag forces educators to act as de facto policymakers, creating a fragmented landscape where student protections vary significantly depending on local governance rather than universal safety standards.

1.3.2 The Digital Divide and Infrastructural Inequity

Beyond ethical risks, the integration of AI in K–12 education exacerbates existing systemic inequities known as the digital divide (Ahmed, 2024). While AI offers powerful personalized learning tools, access to these technologies is often contingent on financial resources and robust infrastructure. Collie et al. (2024) argue that school-based support serves as a critical job resource; without adequate institutional backing, including access to reliable hardware and paid subscriptions, teachers face high job demands that prevent them from exploring or applying AI. Consequently, students in affluent districts gain early proficiency in prompt engineering and advanced computational problem-solving, while those in low-income districts are often relegated to using older, less capable, or ad-supported versions of these tools. Andrejevic and Selwyn (2020) warn that this disparity may lead to a "cascading logic of automation"

(p. 123) where cash-strapped schools are forced to implement automated systems to replace human labor for efficiency, whereas well-funded schools utilize AI to augment human creativity and mentorship.

This infrastructural limitation risks widening the achievement gap into a permanent AI literacy gap. Kalyani et al. (2025) emphasize that the majority of current research focuses on well-resourced regions, leaving a critical gap in understanding how AI tools can be successfully adapted for rural and underserved areas where reliable high-speed internet is often absent. The lack of connectivity effectively excludes these communities from the educational opportunities cloud-based AI systems provide. Furthermore, Viberg et al. (2025) highlight that countries and regions vary significantly in their AI Readiness, suggesting that infrastructural inequity is a structural barrier that dictates which educators can effectively access and trust these technologies. Unless addressed, these disparities ensure that the benefits of AI-augmented learning remain unequally distributed based on socioeconomic status.

1.3.3 Teacher Readiness and Professional Development Gaps

As AI technologies rapidly enter K–12 classrooms, many teachers are excited about the potential but unsure how to use them effectively (Kelley & Wenzel, 2025). This challenge is not rooted in resistance but in a lack of formal preparation and relevant support. Most teacher preparation programs do not prepare educators to use AI in the field providing very little exposure to AI tools, concepts, or ethical considerations (Cheah et al., 2025; Durrani et al., 2024; Sperling et al., 2024). Teachers may be encountering GenAI through headlines or student use of tools like ChatGPT rather than in focused PD programs. Naturally, this lack of exposure contributes to hesitation and inconsistent classroom use. In-service PD on AI remains rare and unevenly distributed. While a few districts provide structured training, many teachers must rely on informal learning or personal experimentation (Velander et al., 2024). Moreover, much of the current PD programs are overly generic, focusing on "what AI is" or how to operate a tool, rather than how to use AI meaningfully to support instruction (Li et al., 2025). Teachers need support in real-world contexts: How can AI enhance student inquiry? When should it be limited or avoided? How do we navigate ethical risks like plagiarism or algorithmic bias?

Additionally, research indicates that the effectiveness of AI tools depends critically on teacher agency and preparation. Technology by itself does not magically improve learning—it's how educators integrate AI that makes the difference in student learning. For instance, Collie et al. (2024) found a strong link between teachers' GenAI self-efficacy and their ability to meaningfully integrate AI into instruction. This study highlights that lower confidence limits use to administrative or planning tasks instead of active classroom application. A study by Cheah et al. (2025) is consistent with these findings: a significant majority of K–12 teachers surveyed in this study reported feeling "not at all" or only "slightly" prepared to implement GenAI tools, underscoring widespread unpreparedness. It's also clear that AI self-efficacy varies notably by prior technology experience and school-based support structures. Bergdahl and Sjöberg (2025) observed that educators with access to institutional resources and supportive leadership felt more confident exploring AI use in instruction, whereas others lacked opportunity to build such skills. Qualitative research involving 66 teachers across disciplines in Turkey further corroborates that perceived control and school culture shape readiness to adopt AI-enhanced teaching practices (Filiz et al., 2025). To move beyond passive use toward pedagogical co-creation with AI, PD programs must be substantial, hands-on, and sustained. One promising model involves self-directed use of GenAI tools like ChatGPT for lesson planning empowering teachers to experiment, reflect, and iterate as part of their instructional growth. This approach aligns with recommendations from broader research emphasizing the need for collaborative design, pilot implementation, and reflective practice as core elements of PD that build agency alongside technical competence (Lin & Van Brummelen, 2021).

In summary, research highlights the importance of sustained and embedded teacher professional learning focused on AI. Teachers benefit from ongoing support that includes ethical inquiry, curriculum alignment, and hands-on practice with AI tools. Research findings indicate that successful PD programs cover not just how to use AI technologies, but also how to critically evaluate AI recommendations and data practices in the classroom (Tan et al., 2025), and may include co-learning models where teachers and students explore AI together as partners (McLeod & Richardson, 2023). However, the human teacher remains central: AI can free up teachers from some routine tasks and provide actionable data, but it's the teacher's expertise and empathy that turn those into meaningful learning experiences for students.

1.3.4 Over-Reliance and Deskilling

Even when teachers are ready and trained, the design and deployment of AI systems can still undermine their professional role (Röhl, 2025). A growing concern in the education field is that over-automation, especially in instructional decision-making, risks shifting authority from teachers to algorithms. In this model, teachers become "machine minders," tasked with monitoring students and systems, rather than making instructional decisions themselves (Merikko & Kivimäki, 2022). This erosion of agency often stems from black-box AI tools that offer decisions or recommendations with no explanation (Gillani et al., 2023). If a dashboard suggests a student re-do a lesson, a teacher may feel pressured to comply even if they know the student understood the concept (Viberg et al., 2025). Over time, this undermines the practice of teaching as an art of nuance, judgment, and responsiveness (Zhai, 2025). Teachers who defer too frequently to AI outputs may find fewer opportunities to adapt instruction, mentor students, or critically reflect on learning outcomes (Kizilcec, 2024).

The risk of over-reliance extends critically to students, posing significant cognitive risks to their intellectual development. As GenAI tools become capable of drafting essays, solving equations, and summarizing texts instantly, there is a danger that students will offload the productive struggle essential for deep learning. If students routinely rely on AI to generate ideas or structure arguments, they may bypass the cognitive processes required to develop critical thinking, resilience, and original expression (Zhai, 2025). This 'cognitive offloading' can inhibit the development of metacognitive skills, such as the ability to monitor and regulate one's own thinking, and lead to deskilling or a loss of core proficiencies (Fowlin et al., 2025). Furthermore, students developing their worldview are particularly vulnerable to the subtle hallucinations and biases inherent in Large Language Models (LLMs). Without strong epistemological scaffolding, young learners may accept AI-generated misinformation as fact, compromising their ability to discern truth and engage in rigorous inquiry (Gillani et al., 2023).This risk is most acute in under-resourced schools, where educators face high workloads and limited support. In these settings, AI tools may be adopted not to enhance instruction, but to alleviate labor shortages. When teachers are stretched thin, they may accept AI-generated grades, groupings, or feedback at face value simply because there's no time to verify them. This isn't a failure of individual teachers, it's a systems-level failure to safeguard human agency in technology adoption. Yet this outcome is not inevitable. AI tools can be designed with co-agency in mind, where the system augments teacher judgment rather than replaces it (Darling-Hammond & Oakes, 2021). This requires systems that are explainable (teachers understand the "why" behind a recommendation), flexible (teachers can override or adapt outputs), and collaborative (AI provides data, but the teacher drives interpretation). For example, an AI might flag a drop in performance, but the teacher adjusts the teaching strategies knowing the student was recently absent. Most importantly, teachers must be at the frontline of shaping these tools. Co-designing AI systems with educators ensures that their professional knowledge is embedded in how the tools function. When AI serves as a partner, not a decision-maker, it can free teachers to focus more on what they do best: building relationships, nurturing thinking, and adapting learning to students' needs (Bulathwela et al., 2021; Fowlin et al., 2025).

1.3.5 Conclusions

In a rapidly evolving AI-driven landscape, schools hold a vital responsibility to prepare students not only to *use* AI tools, but to *understand, question, and shape* the systems that increasingly influence their lives (Gu & Ericson, 2025). Without a coherent and multidimensional approach to AI literacy, K–12 education risks deepening inequities, limiting civic participation, and weakening students' capacity to thrive in an AI-driven society.

As research findings demonstrate, AI can personalize learning, support inclusive classrooms, and ignite ethical inquiry, but that happens only when AI is implemented with intentionality, transparency, and a sustained commitment to equity. Realizing the potential of AI-enhanced education requires more than access to technology; it demands teacher readiness, thoughtful pedagogy, and continuous professional learning. Educators must be equipped to integrate AI critically, model responsible and reflective use, and guide students in navigating the complex ethical and societal questions that accompany intelligent technologies (Owoc et al., 2021). AI literacy, therefore, must become a core competency not only for students, but for the entire education system (Gu & Ericson, 2025).

As AI systems grow more capable and pervasive, they are reshaping the very skills, dispositions, and literacies people, especially young learners, need to thrive in a digitally mediated world. A growing consensus affirms that conceptual AI knowledge should be part of *general education*, not reserved for specialists (Zhou et al., 2020). AI literacy now stands alongside other essential 21st-century skills. Yet, education has struggled to keep pace with these rapid, AI-driven changes. Students regularly interact with AI, through chatbot homework helpers, algorithmically curated feeds, and adaptive learning platforms, but these experiences are often unstructured and lack critical scaffolding. Despite living amid AI technologies like Siri and Alexa, there remains a growing literacy gap in young people's understanding of the assumptions and algorithms behind these systems (Su & Zhong, 2022). Bridging this gap is no longer optional; it is a civic, ethical, and educational imperative.

References

Andrejevic, M., & Selwyn, N. (2020). Facial recognition technology in schools: Critical questions and concerns. *Learning, Media, and Technology, 45*(2), 115–128. https://doi.org/10.1080/17439884.2020.1686014

Ahmed, F. (2024). The digital divide and AI in education: Addressing equity and accessibility. *AI EDIFY Journal, 1*(2), 12–23. https://researchcorridor.org/index.php/aiej/article/view/259

Awang, L. A., Yusop, F. D., & Danaee, M. (2025). Current practices and future direction of artificial intelligence in mathematics education: A systematic review. *International Electronic Journal of Mathematics Education, 20*(2), em0823. https://doi.org/10.29333/iejme/16006

Belloula, S. (2025). Empowering educators: Leveraging AI to revolutionize lesson planning. *International Journal of Research in Education and Science, 11*(2), 264–280. https://doi.org/10.46328/ijres.1295

Bentley, S. V. (2025). Knowing you know nothing in the age of generative AI. *Humanities and Social Sciences Communications, 12*, 49. https://doi.org/10.1057/s41599-025-04731-0

Bergdahl, N., & Sjöberg, J. (2025). Attitudes, perceptions and AI self-efficacy in K-12 education. *Computers and Education: Artificial Intelligence, 8*, Article 100358. https://doi.org/10.1016/j.caeai.2024.100358

Bulathwela, S., Pérez-Ortiz, M., Holloway, C., & Shawe-Taylor, J. (2021, December 14). Could AI democratise education? Socio-technical imaginaries of an edtech revolution. In P. R. Diaz, T. Afonja, K. Klemmer, A. Salama, N. Kalavakonda, O. Azeez, & S. Fobi (Eds.), *Proceedings of the 5th workshop on machine learning for the developing world (ML4D) held at NIPS '21:*

The 35th international conference on neural information processing systems. Online . https://doi.org/10.48550/arXiv.2112.02034

Cantú-Ortiz, F. J., Galeano Sánchez, N., Garrido, L., Terashima-Marin, H., & Brena, R. F. (2020). An artificial intelligence educational strategy for the digital transformation. *International Journal on Interactive Design and Manufacturing (IJIDeM), 14*(4), 1195–1209. https://doi.org/10.1007/s12008-020-00702-8

Cheah, Y. H., Lu, J., & Kim, J. (2025). Integrating generative artificial intelligence in K-12 education: Examining teachers' preparedness, practices, and barriers. *Computers and Education: Artificial Intelligence, 8*, Article 100363. https://doi.org/10.1016/j.caeai.2025.100363

Collie, R. J., Martin, A. J., & Gasevic, D. (2024). Teachers' generative AI self-efficacy, valuing, and integration at work: Examining job resources and demands. *Computers and Education: Artificial Intelligence, 7*, Article 100333. https://doi.org/10.1016/j.caeai.2024.100333

Cubio, J. V. (2025). The influence of privacy, bias, and surveillance concerns on teachers' willingness to use artificial intelligence in education. *International Journal of Research and Innovation in Social Science, 9*(3s), 3192–3208. https://doi.org/10.47772/ijriss.2025.903sedu0240

Dai, Y. (2025). Integrating unplugged and plugged activities for holistic AI education: An embodied constructionist pedagogical approach. *Education and Information Technologies, 30*(5), 6741–6764. https://doi.org/10.1007/s10639-024-13043-w

Darling-Hammond, L., & Oakes, J. (2021). *Preparing teachers for deeper learning*. Harvard Education Press.

Demszky, D., Liu, J., Hill, H.C., Jurafsky, D., & Piech, D.C. (2023). *Can automated feedback improve teachers' uptake of student ideas? Evidence from a randomized controlled trial in a large-scale online course*. (EdWorkingPaper 21–483). Annenberg Institute at Brown University. https://doi.org/10.26300/thn9-wh86

Durrani, R., Iqbal, A., & Akram, H. (2024). Artificial intelligence (AI) in early childhood education, exploring challenges, opportunities and future directions: A scoping review. *Qlantic Journal of Social Sciences, 5*(2), 411–423.https://doi.org/10.55737/qjss.135537445

Fan, H., Chen, G., Wang, X., & Peng, Z. (2024). LessonPlanner: Assisting novice teachers to prepare pedagogy-driven lesson plans with large language models. In L. Yao, M. Goel, A. Ion, & P. Lopes (Eds.) *Proceedings of the 37th Annual ACM Symposium on user interface software and technology* (pp. 1–20). Association for Computing Machinery. https://doi.org/10.1145/3654777.3676390

Federal Trade Commission. (n.d.). *Children's online privacy protection rule (COPPA)*. Author. https://www.ftc.gov/legal-library/browse/rules/childrens-online-privacy-protection-rule-coppa

Filiz, O., Kaya, M. H., & Adiguzel, T. (2025). Teachers and AI: Understanding the factors influencing AI integration in K-12 education. *Education and Information Technology, 30*(13), 17931–17967. https://doi.org/10.1007/s10639-025-13463-2

Fowlin, J., Coleman, D., Ryan, S., Gallo, C., Soares, E., & Hazelton, N. (2025). Empowering educators: Operationalizing age-old learning principles using AI. *Education Sciences, 15*(3), 393. https://doi.org/10.3390/educsci15030393

Gagné, R. M., Briggs, L. J., & Wager, W. W. (1992). *Principles of instructional design (4th ed.)*. Harcourt Brace Jovanovich College Publishers.

Gillani, N., Eynon, R., Chiabaut, C., & Finkel, K. (2023). Unpacking the "Black Box" of AI in education. *Educational Technology & Society, 26*(1), 99–111. https://doi.org/10.30191/ets.202301_26(1).0008

Gu, X., & Ericson, B. J. (2025). AI literacy in K-12 and higher education in the wake of generative AI: An integrative review. In L. Porter, N. Brown, B. Morrison, & C.S. Montero (Eds.) *Proceedings of the 2025 ACM Conference on International Computing Education Research* (vol. 1, pp. 125–140). Association for Computing Machinery. https://doi.org/10.1145/3702652.3744217

Halkiopoulos, C., & Gkintoni, E. (2024). Leveraging AI in e-learning: Personalized learning and adaptive assessment through cognitive neuropsychology—A systematic analysis. *Electronics, 13*(18), 3762. https://doi.org/10.3390/electronics13183762

Holmes, W., & Porayska-Pomsta, K. (Eds.). (2023). *The ethics of artificial intelligence in education.* Routledge.

Kalyani, K., Praveen Kumar, T. D., & Roopa, A. N. (2025) AI-based tools for enhancing reflective practice and self-efficacy in pre-service teachers. *The Scientific Temper, 16*(4), 4128–4135. https://scientifictemper.com/index.php/tst/article/view/1932

Kelley, M., & Wenzel, T. (2025). Advancing artificial intelligence literacy in teacher education through professional partnership inquiry. *Education Sciences, 15*(6), 659. https://doi.org/10.3390/educsci15060659

Kestin, G., Miller, K., Klales, A., Milbourne, T., & Ponti, G. (2025). AI tutoring outperforms in-class active learning: An RCT introducing a novel research-based design in an authentic educational setting. *Scientific Reports, 15*, 17458. https://doi.org/10.1038/s41598-025-97652-6

Kizilcec, R. F. (2024). To advance AI use in education, focus on understanding educators. *International Journal of Artificial Intelligence in Education, 34*(1), 12–19. https://doi.org/10.1007/s40593-023-00351-4

Kumari, D. A., Begum, D. S., Paunikar, M. S., Kaur, A. & Verma, D. S. (2025). The role of artificial intelligence in teacher training: Enhancing pedagogical effectiveness. *Journal of Marketing & Social Research, 2*(5), 116–122. https://doi.org/10.61336/jmsr/25-05-13

Lee, S. J., & Kwon, K. (2024). A systematic review of AI education in K–12 classrooms from 2018 to 2023: Topics, strategies, and learning outcomes. *Computers and Education: Artificial Intelligence, 6*, Article 100211. https://doi.org/10.1016/j.caeai.2024.100211

Li, M., & Wilson, J. (2025). AI-integrated scaffolding to enhance agency and creativity in K-12 English Language Learners: A Systematic review. *Information, 16*(7), 519. https://doi.org/10.3390/info16070519

Li, Z., Wang, C., & Bonk, C. J. (2025). Generative AI for teachers' self-directed professional development: A mixed-methods study. *TechTrends*. https://doi.org/10.1007/s11528-025-01123-8

McLeod, A., & Richardson, H. (2023). Co-constructing skills for ChatGPT at university. *Journal of Academic Language and Learning, 17*(1), T70–T80. https://journal.aall.org.au/index.php/jall/article/view/929.

McStay, A., & Rosner, G. (2021). Emotional artificial intelligence in children's toys and devices: Ethics, governance and practical remedies. *Big Data & Society, 8*(1), 2053951721994877. https://doi.org/10.1177/2053951721994877

Merikko, J., & Kivimäki, V. (2022). "Replacing teachers? Doubt it." Practitioners' views on adaptive learning technologies' impact on the teaching profession. *Frontiers in Education, 7*, 1010255. https://doi.org/10.3389/feduc.2022.1010255

National Foundation for Educational Research. (2024). *ChatGPT in lesson preparation: Teacher choices trial: Evaluation report*. Education Endowment Foundation. https://educationendowmentfoundation.org.uk/projects-and-evaluation/projects/chatgpt-in-lesson-preparation-teacher-choices-trial

Owoc, M. L., Sawicka, A., & Weichbroth, P. (2021). Artificial intelligence technologies in education: Benefits, challenges and strategies of implementation. In M.L. Owoc, & M. Pondel (Eds.), *Artificial Intelligence for Knowledge Management. AI4KM 2019.* (vol. 599, pp. 37–58). IFIP Advances in Information and Communication Technology. Springer. https://doi.org/10.1007/978-3-030-85001-2_4

Panaoura, R. (2025). Teaching mathematics in the artificial intelligence era: Challenges and concerns in higher education. *Social Education Research, 6*(2), 242–249. https://doi.org/10.37256/ser.6220256730

Rafner, J., Zana, B., Bang Hansen, I., Ceh, S., Sherson, J., Benedek, M., & Lebuda, I. (2025). Agency in human-AI collaboration for image generation and creative writing: Preliminary insights from think-aloud protocols. *Creativity Research Journal*, 1–24. https://doi.org/10.1080/10400419.2025.2587803

Ravi, P., Masla, J., Kakoti, G., Lin, G. C., Anderson, E., Taylor, M., Ostrowski, A. K., Breazeal, C., Klopfer, E., & Abelson, H. (2025). Co-designing large language model tools for project-based learning with K12 educators. In N. Yamashita, V. Evers, K. Yatani, X. Ding, B. Lee, M. Chetty, P. Toups-Dugas (Eds.), *Proceedings of the 2025 CHI conference on human factors in computing systems* (Article 138, pp. 1–25). Association for Computing Machinery. https://doi.org/10.1145/3706598.3713971

Röhl, T. (2025). Machine teaching? Teachers' professional agency in the age of algorithmic tools in education. *British Journal of Sociology of Education,* 1–15. https://doi.org/10.1080/01425692.2025.2495625

Salas-Pilco, S. Z., Xiao, K., & Hu, X. (2022). Artificial intelligence and learning analytics in teacher education: A systematic review. *Education Sciences, 13*(9), 897. https://doi.org/10.3390/educsci12080569

Salloum, S. A., Alomari, K. M., Alfaisal, A. M., Aljanada, R. A., & Basiouni, A. (2025). Emotion recognition for enhanced learning: Using AI to detect students' emotions and adjust teaching methods. *Smart Learning Environments, 12*, 21. https://doi.org/10.1186/s40561-025-00374-5

Schiff, D. (2022). Education for AI, not AI for education: The role of education and ethics in national AI policy strategies. *International Journal of Artificial Intelligence in Education, 32*(3), 527–563. https://doi.org/10.1007/s40593-021-00270-2

Schlund, R., & Zitek, E. M. (2024). Algorithmic versus human surveillance leads to lower perceptions of autonomy and increased resistance. *Communications Psychology, 2*, 53. https://doi.org/10.1038/s44271-024-00102-8

Sperling, K., Stenberg, C.-J., McGrath, C., Åkerfeldt, A., Heintz, F., & Stenliden, L. (2024). In search of artificial intelligence (AI) literacy in teacher education: A scoping review. *Computers and Education Open, 6*, Article 100169. https://doi.org/10.1016/j.caeo.2024.100169

Su, J., & Zhong, Y. (2022). Artificial intelligence (AI) in early childhood education: Curriculum design and future directions. *Computers and Education: Artificial Intelligence, 3*, Article 100072. https://doi.org/10.1016/j.caeai.2022.100072

Suryani, M., Sensuse, D. I., Santoso, H. B., Aji, R. F., Hadi, S., Suryono, R. R., & Kautsarina, K. (2024). An initial user model design for adaptive interface development in learning management system based on cognitive load. *Cognition, technology & work, 26*(4), 653–672. https://doi.org/10.1007/s10111-024-00772-8

Tan, X., Cheng, G., & Ling, M. H. (2025). Artificial intelligence in teaching and teacher professional development: A systematic review. *Computers and Education: Artificial Intelligence, 8*, Article 100355. https://doi.org/10.1016/j.caeai.2024.100355

U.S. Department of Education. (n.d.). *Protecting student privacy: Family educational rights and privacy act (FERPA).* Student Privacy Policy Office. https://studentprivacy.ed.gov/

Lin, P., & Van Brummelen, J. (2021). Engaging teachers to co-design integrated AI curriculum for K–12 classrooms. In Y. Kitamura, A. Quigley, K. Isbister, T. Igarashi, P. Bjørn,, & S. Drucker (Eds.) *Proceedings of the 2021 CHI Conference on human factors in computing systems.* (Article 239, pp. 1–12). Association for Computing Machinery. https://doi.org/10.1145/3411764.3445377

Velander, J., Taiye, M. A., Otero, N., & Milrad, M. (2024). Artificial intelligence in K-12 education: Eliciting and reflecting on Swedish teachers' understanding of AI and its implications for teaching & learning. *Education and Information Technologies, 29*(4), 4085–4105. https://doi.org/10.1007/s10639-023-11990-4

Viberg, O., Cukurova, M., Feldman-Maggor, Y., Alexandron, G., Shirai, S., Kanemune, S., Wasson, B., Tømte, C., Spikol, D., Milrad, M., Coelho, R., & Kizilcec, R. F. (2025). What explains teachers' trust in AI in education across six countries? *International Journal of Artificial Intelligence in Education, 35*(3), 1288–1316. https://doi.org/10.1007/s40593-024-00433-x

Zha, S., Qiao, Y., Hu, Q., Li, Z., Gong, J., & Xu, Y. (2024). Designing child-centric AI learning environments: Insights from LLM-enhanced creative project-based learning. *International Journal of Human-Computer Studies, 204*, Article 103602. https://doi.org/10.1016/j.ijhcs.2025.103602

Zhai, X. (2025). Transforming teachers' roles and agencies in the era of generative AI: Perceptions, acceptance, knowledge, and practices. *Journal of Science Education and Technology, 34*(6), 1323–1333. https://doi.org/10.1007/s10956-024-10174-0

Zhou, X., Van Brummelen, J., & Lin, P. (2020). *Designing AI learning experiences for K-12: Emerging works, future opportunities and a design framework.* (arXiv:2009.10228). arXiv. https://doi.org/10.48550/arXiv.2009.10228

Chapter 2
AI Literacy Education

Abstract This chapter establishes the theoretical foundation for integrating Artificial Intelligence (AI) literacy across K–12 curricula. We conduct a systematic, comparative review of six highly influential AI literacy frameworks, including models from AI4K12, UNESCO, and Digital Promise, to determine a consistent and developmentally appropriate definition. The analysis reveals a strong consensus on a multidimensional model balancing foundational technical knowledge (Understand), critical reasoning (Evaluate), and responsible application (Use). Despite this conceptual clarity, our subsequent review of existing K–12 curriculum examples identifies critical implementation challenges. Current efforts are fragmented, often confined to computer science electives or extracurricular programs, lacking the necessary alignment and scalability for widespread integration. This fragmentation is compounded by a persistent pedagogical deficit, where theoretical frameworks fail to provide teachers with explicit, actionable guidance for integrating AI concepts across diverse subjects. We conclude by formally adopting the multidimensional AI literacy model and establishing the urgent need for a research-informed pedagogical framework to guide effective, equitable, and sustainable cross-disciplinary instruction.

2.1 Introduction

In the previous chapter we established the need for AI literacy education. Today, ensuring that all learners, particularly those in K–12 settings, develop a foundational understanding of AI is not simply a matter of digital fluency, but a prerequisite for future-ready citizenship, ethical reasoning, and economic opportunity. We define future-ready citizenship not merely as technical preparedness, but as the possession of adaptive competencies, specifically critical thinking, digital agency, and complex problem-solving, that allow individuals to navigate and shape indeterminate futures. This alignment draws on global frameworks such as the OECD Learning Compass 2030 and UNESCO's Futures of Education, which emphasize that education must equip learners to reconcile tensions, take responsibility, and mobilize knowledge in

I. Lyublinskaya and X. Du, *A Pedagogical Framework for K–12 AI Literacy*, Springer Texts in Education, https://doi.org/10.1007/978-3-032-23570-1_2

evolving sociotechnical contexts (OECD, 2019; Miao & Cukurova, 2024; Miao et al., 2024).

In this chapter we examine the existing AI literacy frameworks and curricula to build a foundation for pedagogical action. We begin by reviewing established AI literacy frameworks from the academic literature, critically analyzing their scope, focus, and applicability to the K–12 environment. This analysis will highlight the various conceptualizations of AI literacy—from technical understanding to ethical and societal awareness. Subsequently, we will examine current K–12 AI literacy curriculum examples, identifying common content themes, instructional methodologies, and potential gaps in existing approaches, particularly concerning cross-disciplinary integration.

Through this analytical synthesis, the chapter identifies core competencies necessary for AI literacy, explores developmental and disciplinary considerations, and surfaces tensions between competing visions (e.g., technical versus civic orientations) that complicate curricular design. The analysis also draws attention to the limited, often fragmented pedagogical guidance available to support effective implementation in everyday classrooms. This comprehensive review culminates in the chapter's conclusion: the proposal of a multidimensional definition of AI literacy that is both developmentally appropriate and pedagogically actionable. It is this foundational definition that necessitates and calls for the creation of a coherent, research-informed pedagogical framework that can guide curriculum development, instructional design, and educator professional learning ensuring that AI literacy becomes an integral, equitable, and empowering part of K–12 education.

2.2 AI Literacy Frameworks for K–12 Education

To inform the development of a pedagogical approach, we conducted a targeted review of the literature to identify the most prominent models currently shaping the field. We selected six highly influential frameworks based on three primary inclusion criteria: (1) high citation impact within academic literature; (2) widespread adoption by international policy bodies (e.g., UNESCO, OECD); and (3) specific relevance to K–12 implementation. While numerous emerging models exist, we excluded frameworks that were purely technical, focused exclusively on higher education or those lacking broad empirical or policy validation to focus on the dominant paradigms defining the current landscape. This selection includes *Five Big Ideas in AI* framework (Touretzky et al., 2023) for its definitive focus on core computational content standards; the AI competencies framework by Long and Magerko (2020) for grounding the discussion in essential skills and design; the *UNESCO AI Competency Framework for Students* (Miao et al., 2024) for its essential global perspective on ethical and societal impact; the multidimensional model for AI literacy suggested by Ng et al. (2024) for the focus on holistic, affective dimensions; the OECD *AI Literacy Framework* (OECD, 2025) for its emphasis on educational policy and curricular integration; and finally, the *AI Literacy: A Framework to Understand, Evaluate, and*

Use Emerging Technology (Mills et al., 2024) for its practitioner-focused structure. By comparing these diverse approaches to AI literacy, we aim to balance technical understanding, critical evaluation, and responsible use necessary for future-ready citizenship, leading to the selection of a framework best suited for broad curricular integration.

We analyze each framework across four key dimensions, derived from the core needs established in the previous chapter (e.g., citizenship, ethical reasoning, cross-disciplinary relevance). These analytical criteria are: (1) Scope and focus, determining whether the primary emphasis is technical (the "how"), ethical/civic (the "should"), or user-centric application (the "use"); (2) K–12 applicability, assessing the presence of clear, developmentally appropriate guidance across different grade bands; (3) Potential for cross-disciplinary integration, evaluating how easily the framework translates beyond specialized computer science instruction; and (4) Pedagogical feasibility, judging the extent to which the framework offers explicit guidance and support for classroom instruction and teacher professional learning. This structured comparison will highlight the conceptual strengths across the field while identifying the remaining gaps in pedagogical implementation.

The Five Big Ideas in AI framework (Touretzky et al., 2023) serves as the foundational standard for technical content in K–12 AI education, particularly within the United States. The framework is structured around five core conceptual ideas—Perception, Representation & Reasoning, Learning, Natural Interaction, and Societal Impact—each broken down into specific learning progressions across grade bands (K-12). The strength of this framework lies in its clarity regarding what technical concepts students must know, providing a definitive approach to demystify AI mechanisms like machine learning and data-driven reasoning. However, when assessed against our criteria, its weakness emerges in its pedagogical feasibility for broad integration. As a standards-based model rooted in computer science education, it primarily functions as a content guide.

The seminal work by Long and Magerko (2020), which proposes AI literacy as a set of competencies, represents a shift in the discourse from technical content toward user-centric skills. Their highly influential definition centers on the individual's ability to critically evaluate AI technologies, communicate and collaborate effectively with AI, and use AI as a tool in diverse contexts. The strength of this framework lies in its rigor as the academic cornerstone for defining AI literacy through a practical, functional lens, anchoring the discussion firmly in necessary skills for future citizenship.

The UNESCO AI Competency Framework (Miao et al., 2024) offers a necessary global and humanistic counterpoint to the technical and national frameworks. Its central focus is on promoting AI literacy grounded in principles of human rights, inclusivity, equity, and sustainability, prioritizing the ethical and societal dimensions. Structured around four core dimensions for students—Human-Centered Mindset, Ethics of AI, AI Techniques and Applications, and AI System Design—and categorized across three progression levels (Understand, Apply, Create), its strength lies in establishing a non-negotiable ethical foundation for future citizens and co-creators of AI.

The multidimensional model for AI literacy proposed by Ng and colleagues (Ng et al., 2024) significantly advances the conceptualization of AI literacy by moving beyond purely cognitive and technical domains to propose a multidimensional model encompassing Affective, Behavioral, Cognitive, and Ethical (ABCE) factors. The distinct strength of this model lies in its focus on the Affective components, such as self-efficacy, interest, and attitudes toward AI, which are crucial predictors of student engagement and lifelong learning that are often omitted from standards-based frameworks. By including behavioral dimensions (e.g., active collaboration with AI tools and reflective habits), Ng et al. provide a holistic lens for understanding how students adopt and interact with AI in practice.

The OECD AI Literacy Framework for Primary and Secondary Education [AILit] (OECD, 2025), developed with major international partners, serves as the primary policy-driven model for curricular integration. Structurally comprehensive, AILit outlines four core domains—Engage with AI, Create with AI, Manage AI, and Design AI—with detailed competencies structured for primary and secondary education. Its distinct strength lies in its explicit connection to educational policy and assessment, making it highly influential in setting international benchmarks for K–12 student competency. Furthermore, AILit explicitly promotes cross-disciplinary integration by providing learning scenarios for subjects outside of computer science, such as using AI for statistical analysis in mathematics or evaluating sources in social studies.

The Digital Promise framework (Mills et al., 2024), structured around three core modes of engagement—Understand, Evaluate, and Use—represents the most advanced synthesis of AI literacy concepts into a practitioner-focused and highly adaptable K–12 model. Its core strength lies in balancing the need for technical awareness (drawing from the Five Big Ideas in AI framework) with a strong emphasis on core values like human judgment and centering justice, thereby fulfilling the ethical and civic mandates stressed by UNESCO. This structure inherently boosts its pedagogical feasibility, as the three modes provide clear, functional objectives for teachers regardless of their technical expertise. The framework excels at translating complex competencies into actionable steps for critical evaluation and responsible tool use, making it the most immediate guide for teachers seeking to engage students with present-day AI.

The review of these six core AI literacy frameworks reveals a significant consensus regarding the necessary scope of AI literacy: it must integrate foundational technical understanding (Five Big Ideas in AI), critical evaluation skills (Long & Magerko), and ethical reasoning (UNESCO). Frameworks like Digital Promise and OECD successfully synthesize these dimensions into actionable, user-centric modes of engagement, providing a strong conceptual foundation for K–12 educators. However, even within these practitioner-oriented models, a recurrent limitation is the lack of a coherent, validated pedagogical methodology for non-specialist teachers. While offering partial scaffolding, these frameworks primarily define the what and, in some cases, the why, but they stop short of offering the comprehensive, subject-specific guidance on how to achieve cross-disciplinary integration in everyday lessons. This observation aligns with empirical analysis of national AI strategies, which found that policymakers overwhelmingly prioritize workforce training ("Education for AI") while neglecting the pedagogical guidelines needed to implement tools effectively in classrooms ("AI for Education") (Schiff, 2022). Furthermore, implementation studies caution that without such theory-based scaffolding and instructional design, teachers struggle to move students beyond superficial tool use toward deep conceptual competency (Yue et al., 2025; Zhou et al., 2025). This theoretical-to-practice gap establishes the imperative for the following section, which examines current K–12 curriculum examples to determine if practical implementation efforts have successfully bridged this pedagogical deficit.

2.3 Defining the Multidimensional AI Literacy Model

Based on the synthesis of conceptual and practical frameworks, this study adopts a multidimensional model for AI literacy, primarily leveraging the action-oriented structure of the Digital Promise framework (Mills et al., 2024) while incorporating the ethical and developmental depth of UNESCO AI Competency Framework (Miao et al., 2024) and multidimensional model for AI literacy (Ng et al., 2024). This model is defined by three interconnected domains that reflect the necessary balance between technical knowledge, critical evaluation, and practical application for K–12 learners.

2.3.1 Conceptual Knowledge of AI Systems (Understand)

This domain centers on learners' ability to understand what artificial intelligence (AI) is, how it operates, and the core structures behind AI systems. A strong grounding in these ideas—spanning data, algorithmic logic, feedback loops, and the probabilistic nature of AI outputs—is a necessary basis for building both technical fluency and critical awareness. Ng et al. (2024) propose a multidimensional model for AI literacy that emphasizes the need for conceptual understanding as a precursor to effective evaluation and application. They define this domain as encompassing students' ability to distinguish rule-based systems (e.g., if–then logic) from learning-based systems (e.g., machine learning), identify key AI elements such as perception, reasoning, learning, and decision-making, and understand how data, algorithms, and feedback loops interact within these systems. This includes recognizing the probabilistic nature of many AI outputs and the centrality of data in shaping AI behavior. This emphasis aligns with the AI4K12 initiative's Five Big Ideas in AI—Perception; Representation & Reasoning; Learning; Natural Interaction; and Societal Impact—which are widely accepted as organizing principles for AI instruction in the U.S. K–12 education (Touretzky et al., 2019). These big ideas intentionally segment complex AI principles into developmentally appropriate domains: for instance, the idea of 'perception" addresses how sensors enable AI to interpret inputs from the physical and digital environments, while the idea of 'learning' explains how systems evolve through data exposure (Touretzky et al., 2023). International policy bodies like UNESCO and OECD also emphasize foundational AI understanding as a civic competency essential for meaningful participation in AI-mediated societies. These frameworks highlight the importance of competencies such as awareness of uncertainty, computational thinking, data literacy, and critical evaluation of what constitutes human-like intelligence in the AI era (Gu & Ericson, 2025; Miao & Cukurova, 2024; Miao et al., 2024; Zhou et al., 2025).

Despite broad consensus on the importance of conceptual knowledge, many AI education implementations remain fragmented and underdeveloped. Ng et al. (2024) caution that current programs frequently emphasize surface-level facts and isolated activities such as coding tasks or AI tool demonstrations rather than fostering deep, scaffolded conceptual engagement that aligns with students' developmental needs and long-term learning progressions. Their review underscores the lack of coherence across programs and highlights the risk of treating AI literacy as an add-on rather than an integrated domain of study. Lin and Van Brummelen (2021) similarly observed that in K–12 contexts, instructional approaches often prioritized discrete technical skills like basic programming or robotics without sustainable attention to foundational AI concepts or integration of culturally and developmentally responsive pedagogy. Their study that used adaptation of MIT's AI + Ethics curriculum demonstrated that contextualizing AI through hands-on activities and locally relevant scenarios significantly enhanced student engagement and understanding, particularly among underrepresented learners. A systematic review of AI literacy initiatives by Casal-Otero et al. (2023) demonstrated that most of them lack a clearly articulated pedagogical framework. Furthermore, while some programs offer engaging experiential learning opportunities for students, few assess whether students meaningfully grasp AI's underlying principles. The review emphasizes the urgent need for competency-based frameworks that sequence conceptual learning and allow for modular, personalized adaptation to diverse school contexts. Without such structure, AI instruction remains fragmented and inconsistently implemented leaving significant gaps in students' ability to understand, critique, and shape the AI systems that influence their lives. These findings underscore the urgent need to center the 'Understand' domain in curriculum design, ensuring students gain not just exposure to AI tools, but deep, developmentally appropriate understanding of how AI systems work.

2.3.2 *Responsible Application and Collaboration (Use)*

The Use domain of AI literacy refers to students' capacity to meaningfully use, design, iterate on, and reflect upon AI technologies in contextually relevant and ethically informed ways (Long & Magerko, 2020; Mills et al., 2024). This domain encompasses both computational and design fluency, which includes understanding how design choices can affect users differently depending on their identities, needs, and contexts. Given the strategic and ethical nature of AI applications, international organizations now increasingly recognize this domain as essential. UNESCO AI Competency Framework emphasizes the responsible use of AI in education and calls for equipping teachers to address key concerns such as fairness, transparency, and privacy (Miao & Cukurova, 2024). Similarly, the OECD AILit argues that education systems must move beyond basic digital skills to support both students and teachers in effectively managing AI's social and technical implications (OECD, 2025).

In practice, applying AI in K–12 settings includes activities such as using AI-powered language tools, analyzing scientific data with AI-supported platforms, or interacting with intelligent tutoring systems. However, empirical studies caution that meaningful learning occurs only when these tools are embedded within thoughtfully designed, scaffolded learning experiences (Yue et al., 2025; Zhou et al., 2025). Without intentional guidance, students may engage with AI as black box tools, leading to misconceptions or overtrust. Indeed, nearly half of Gen Z youth struggle to recognize that AI systems can produce unreliable outputs, such as fabricating facts or embedding bias, unless explicitly taught otherwise (Zhou et al., 2025).

Design-based learning frameworks have emerged as promising approaches to address this challenge. For example, Yue et al. (2025) propose the "Students as AI Literate Designers" (SAILD) model, where elementary students engage in the creation of AI-infused solutions to real-world problems. Through a structured design cycle—problem framing, ideation, prototyping, and feedback—students develop deeper understandings of how AI systems work and reflect on the impact of their design decisions. This hands-on, iterative learning fosters not only technical fluency but also ethical and civic awareness. The study showed that students in the SAILD program demonstrated measurable gains in AI knowledge, skills, ethical reasoning, and attitudes, illustrating how even young learners can engage in complex AI design tasks when supported by age-appropriate tools and pedagogies.

Global curriculum frameworks reinforce this approach. The OECD AILit framework includes domains such as "Engaging with AI" and "Managing AI's Actions," which require students to critically assess AI system outputs, understand underlying mechanisms, and maintain human oversight (OECD, 2025). Practical initiatives such as TeachAI (a coalition involving Code.org) and AI4All's "AI & Society" workshops further operationalize this domain. These programs provide project-based experiences in which high school students design AI tools for social good or debate real-world ethical dilemmas, such as the use of facial recognition in schools or algorithmic moderation on social media. Early research evidence shows such interventions can meaningfully shift student perspectives: for instance, students became more cautious in trusting AI outputs and more interested in designing equitable technologies after participating in ethical design modules (Ma et al., 2025).

In advocating for a holistic approach to the Use domain, Zhou et al. (2025) explicitly emphasize the importance of including metacognitive and emotional dimensions. They argue that students must reflect on how well their models function, who they benefit, and what assumptions they encode. However, this reflective practice is often underdeveloped in existing programs; their review found only a small number of initiatives explicitly address self-reflection, despite its centrality to lifelong learning and ethical engagement with emerging technologies. As such, the Use domain cannot be reduced to tool usage; rather, it must integrate critical inquiry, social awareness, and design iteration. When students are invited to create with AI in ways that are purposeful, scaffolded, and socially relevant, they begin to see themselves not just as users of technology, but as ethical co-designers of the AI-powered world around them.

2.3.3 Critical Evaluation and Ethical Reasoning (Evaluate)

The Evaluate domain of AI literacy centers on students' capacity to critically assess the ethical, civic, and societal implications of AI. This includes examining pressing issues such as algorithmic bias, fairness, surveillance, data privacy, and the ways AI technologies can perpetuate or challenge systemic inequalities. Ng et al. (2024) argue that AI literacy must extend beyond technical knowledge to encompass ethical discernment and civic awareness, particularly as AI increasingly mediates high-stakes decisions in areas such as education, justice, healthcare, and employment. They emphasize that AI systems should be viewed as sociotechnical constructs shaped by human decisions, values, and power dynamics. This perspective is formalized in the AI4K12 framework, where the Big Idea of Societal Impact introduces students to the broader consequences of AI, including ethical dilemmas and unintended harms. Empirical work by Touretzky et al. (2019) suggests that when these topics are explored through age-appropriate case studies and project-based learning, students can meaningfully engage with complex issues like algorithmic bias and surveillance.

Yang et al. (2025) reinforce this vision, defining AI literacy as a set of competencies that enable individuals to critically evaluate AI technologies, use them effectively, and interact with them responsibly. Their review highlights that evaluation is increasingly being recognized as a foundational skill for navigating AI's influence across various domains of life. However, despite this growing conceptual clarity, there remains a notable gap between aspiration and practice. Kim and Kwon's (2024) systematic review of 36 empirical studies found that K–12 AI education predominantly focused on assessing cognitive outcomes related to machine learning (ML), such as classification, model training, and data input. Specifically, of the 36 studies, only six addressed broader AI literacy goals, including ethical reasoning or societal implications. Most evaluations relied on self-reported surveys or knowledge tests and rarely employed qualitative or mixed-method approaches that could better capture students' reflective thinking or ethical awareness.

This disjuncture reveals the need for more intentional integration of ethical and evaluative dimensions in AI education. A synthesis of literature in the field identifies four key thematic areas that the Evaluate domain should address: (1) algorithmic bias and fairness—such as questioning whether data or models reflect inequities (Miao & Cukurova, 2024); (2) transparency and explainability—understanding how AI makes decisions and why that matters for trust; (3) privacy and data protection—especially relevant in educational settings where AI tools may collect sensitive student data; and (4) the broader societal impact of AI including its influence on autonomy, labor, creativity, misinformation, and democratic engagement. As AI systems become increasingly embedded in classrooms, Gouseti et al. (2025) stress the urgency of developing ethical guidelines that protect student agency and preserve the human elements of teaching and learning. For example, they ask how student autonomy can be maintained if an AI tutoring system prescribes all learning paths, or how the teacher-student relationship evolves in an AI-mediated classroom.

Despite growing awareness of these concerns, empirical research suggests that K–12 AI education still underemphasizes ethical reasoning. Casal-Otero et al. (2023), in a review of AI curricula, found that very few learning experiences explicitly evaluated students' understanding of AI ethics or societal impact. They caution that without thoughtful design, AI education risks overlooking or even reinforcing the very harms it seeks to address. To counter this trend, some curriculum developers have begun to embed ethical inquiry directly into technical lessons. For instance, Lee et al. (2021) implemented AI workshops where students not only built models but also engaged in discussions about bias at every stage of the process. Similarly, the MIT AI + Ethics curriculum (Williams et al., 2019) invites middle school students to train image recognition models and observe how biased versus balanced training data alters performance—prompting inquiry into fairness and representation.

These pedagogical approaches model what many experts advocate: guiding students to ask critical questions about the origins, design, and consequences of AI tools. Questions like "Is this training data representative?", "Who benefits from this AI system?", or "What are the terms of service and privacy implications?" encourage students to connect technical understanding with real-world contexts. In line with this thinking, Yang and Capan (2025), citing findings from an SRI International expert panel, propose that fostering an "AI user identity" should be a central goal of AI literacy—one that cultivates ethical responsibility and a sense of agency. They further argue that an AI-literate learner must not only build and apply AI but also possess the capacity to critically evaluate its risks and benefits from multiple perspectives, including equity, safety, security, and misinformation. This evaluative capacity, they contend, is essential for promoting the safe, responsible, and socially beneficial use of AI.

2.4 Current Status and Gaps in K–12 AI Literacy Curricula

Despite the rapid integration of AI into daily life and the labor market, AI literacy has yet to be systematically embedded into K–12 standard-based curricula at scale. Existing efforts to introduce AI into education are fragmented, often implemented through elective courses, extracurricular programs, or stand-alone units rather than integrated into core subject areas or aligned with national learning standards. This fragmentation presents challenges for ensuring equitable access, developmental coherence, and pedagogical consistency across schools and education systems. A comparative analysis of international initiatives reveals five dominant models of curriculum implementation: discrete, embedded, interdisciplinary, multiple-modality, and flexible. While models like interdisciplinary integration show potential, others—especially discrete and multiple-modality approaches—expose gaps in scalability and pedagogical design.

2.4.1 Limited Integration into Standard-Based Curricula

Across most countries, while efforts to introduce AI literacy are growing, implementation often results in siloed models that fail to integrate into mandatory, standard-based curricula. In nations like the Republic of Korea, proactive policy efforts have led to the development of two elective high school AI subjects—one under the mathematics domain and another within technology and home economics. These courses introduce concepts such as algorithmic thinking, programming, and AI applications through project-based learning. The Seoul Education Office's 2021–2025 AI education plan further promotes AI-integrated electives, with some schools converting up to 15% of class time into AI-focused learning. Despite this progress, these subjects remain elective and are often adopted at the discretion of individual schools or principals, limiting their reach and long-term sustainability (Asia Pacific Foundation of Canada, Korea AI Ethics Association, & Chung-Ang University, 2021). Similarly, Armenia's ICT-based AI curriculum focuses on vocational preparation in the high school grades, aiming to increase technological readiness and direct students toward technical university programs and knowledge-based sectors. However, this model is tightly coupled with economic development goals and remains siloed from broader civic or ethical AI literacy goals, such as media literacy, identity development, or algorithmic accountability (Asia Pacific Foundation of Canada et al., 2021). Other initiatives, such as Intel's AI for Youth and the IBM EdTech Youth Challenge, offer extensive, modular, and age-appropriate content focused on experiential learning. Intel's program, for example, includes 200 h of instruction in three core AI domains—computer vision, natural language processing, and data analysis—culminating in student-designed social impact projects. However, these curricula are typically delivered in after-school settings or specialized AI labs. While they offer flexibility and engagement, they often lack alignment with formal curriculum standards, making it difficult to evaluate student learning outcomes within existing assessment structures (Asia Pacific Foundation of Canada et al., 2021).

2.4.2 *Limited Focus on Pedagogical Integration and Teacher Capacity*

In addition to curricular isolation, there is a notable absence of attention to pedagogical integration strategies and teacher preparation in the design of most AI literacy programs. Kim (2023) analyzes South Korea's K–12 AI curriculum and describes national-scale teacher training programs launched as early as 2020. While these efforts represent a proactive commitment to AI education, the study highlights a persistent lack of unified implementation and integration across schools, with variation in how AI courses are adopted, supported, and connected to broader curricular standards. As documented in a recent systematic review (Viberg et al., 2025), many initiatives focus on exposing students to AI tools and applications without offering guidance on how to teach AI concepts developmentally, ethically, or interdisciplinarily. The majority of PD) opportunities for teachers are one-off, tool-centered workshops rather than sustained, practice-based programs that address core pedagogical challenges, such as designing inquiry-based AI lessons or navigating students' misconceptions about automation and intelligence. Teachers consistently report low confidence in teaching AI—especially when it comes to integrating AI into existing subjects such as math, science, or social studies (Viberg et al., 2025). This gap in teacher readiness is compounded by a lack of scaffolded learning progressions or instructional resources that align AI content with students' cognitive development. For example, most AI curricula are not differentiated by grade level, and few offer specific guidance for supporting diverse learners, such as multilingual students or those with disabilities. Furthermore, the curricular resources often fail to address the ethical and civic dimensions of AI literacy, which are essential for fostering students' critical engagement with AI systems. India's *Let's Learn Artificial Intelligence Step-Up Module* (Atal Innovation Mission, 2025), developed by the Atal Innovation Mission (AIM), provides foundational AI literacy content to over 5,000 Atal Tinkering Labs nationwide. The curriculum includes units on core AI concepts such as computer vision, natural language processing, and ethics, and culminates in project-based activities that aim to build student engagement and technical fluency. However, while the module introduces the concept of ethical AI, it provides limited structured opportunities for students to critically examine algorithmic bias, the social consequences of model outputs, or to reflect on their digital agency. These limitations show a broader challenge in global AI education: many entry-level AI programs focus on technical skills without embedding systematic approaches to support critical thinking, civic reasoning, or ethical reflection.

2.4.3 *Early Examples of Cross-Disciplinary AI Integration*

Some innovative models show potential for interdisciplinary integration. For instance, Canada's Yukon Territory Applied Design, Skills and Technologies curriculum (British Columbia Ministry of Education and Child Care, n.d.) integrates AI-related problem-solving within a broader design and community-oriented learning framework. Students explore design thinking through culturally responsive activities, such as studying traditional Yukon shelters, which connects technical learning to social responsibility and Indigenous knowledge. Likewise, Qatar's Computing and Information Technology curriculum adopts a dual-track approach that balances technical depth with broader applications in information systems (Ministry of Education & Higher Education, State of Qatar, 2018). These cases demonstrate that AI literacy can be woven into cross-cutting themes like sustainability, ethics, or systems thinking—but such models remain rare and under-researched. What is lacking across the board is a coherent pedagogical framework that (1) connects AI content to existing learning goals across subjects; (2) supports educators in facilitating conceptual, inquiry-driven, and reflective learning; and (3) builds developmental progressions that span K–12 levels.

2.5 Toward a Pedagogical Framework for AI Literacy Integration

Few K–12 curricula provide opportunities for students to examine how AI systems work, what data they rely on, or how they might reproduce existing inequalities. Instead, most AI-related education efforts focus narrowly on technical skill-building—such as coding and robotics—which are valuable but insufficient for fostering a deeper, multidimensional understanding of AI's societal impact (Sperling et al., 2025). Research consistently demonstrates that AI literacy curricula predominantly emphasize technical knowledge, with far less attention to critical, situated, and ethical perspectives on AI. A future-ready education system must therefore go beyond technical skill-building to encompass the civic, ethical, and humanistic dimensions of AI. This includes helping students recognize algorithmic bias, understand how AI systems make decisions, explore their personal and societal implications, and reflect on the role of human judgment in an increasingly automated world (Ng et al., 2024).

The current landscape points to a clear and urgent need: a research-informed pedagogical framework for AI literacy integration in K–12 education. Though the review established the multidimensional definition of AI literacy (Understand, Evaluate, Use), the curriculum review confirms the persistent pedagogical deficit in practice. To effectively bridge the divide between ethical principles and classroom realities, this framework must move beyond abstract principles or one-off interventions. It needs to provide explicit support for actionable curriculum design that connects AI concepts to core disciplinary standards; developmentally appropriate instructional strategies that facilitate conceptual, inquiry-driven, and reflective learning; and inclusive assessment tools that recognize diverse ways of demonstrating AI literacy across age and context. The next chapter presents the design and theoretical development of the Pedagogical Framework for AI Literacy Integration. This framework is explicitly constructed to address the limitations identified here, providing educators with the necessary structure and actionable guidance to achieve systematic, cross-disciplinary AI literacy throughout the K–12 curriculum.

References

Asia Pacific Foundation of Canada, Korea AI Ethics Association, Humanities Research Institute, & Chung-Ang University. (2021). *Talent for the future: AI education for K–12 in Canada and South Korea.* Asia Pacific Foundation of Canada. https://www.asiapacific.ca/publication/ai-education-k-12-canada-and-south-korea.

Atal Innovation Mission (AIM), Government of India. (2025). *Let's learn Artificial Intelligence: Step-up module.* NITI Aayog. https://www.scribd.com/document/475299735/Lets-learn-AI-StepUp-Module-NITI-AAYOG

British Columbia Ministry of Education and Child Care (n.d.) *Digital literacy and the use of AI in education: supports for British Columbia schools.* B.C. Curriculum. https://www2.gov.bc.ca/gov/content/education-training/k-12/administration/program-management/ai-in-education

Casal-Otero, L., Catala, A., Fernández-Morante, C., Taboada, M., Cebreiro, B., & Barro, S. (2023). AI literacy in K-12: A systematic literature review. *International Journal of STEM Education, 10*(1), 29. https://doi.org/10.1186/s40594-023-00418-7

Gouseti, A., James, F., Fallin, L., & Burden, K. (2025). The ethics of using AI in K-12 education: A systematic literature review. *Technology, Pedagogy and Education, 34*(2), 161–182. https://doi.org/10.1080/1475939X.2024.2428601

Gu, X., & Ericson, B. J. (2025). AI literacy in K-12 and Higher Education in the wake of Generative AI: An integrative review. [Preprint].arXiv. https://doi.org/10.48550/arXiv.2503.00079.

Kim, D. H. (2023). AI curriculum design for Korea K–12 AI education through analyzing AI education curriculum. *International Journal of Recent Technology and Engineering, 12(*3), 113–120. https://doi.org/10.35940/ijrte.C7860.0912323

Kim, K., & Kwon, K. (2024). *A systematic review of evaluation in K–12 artificial intelligence education from 2013 to 2022.* Advance online publication. https://doi.org/10.1080/10494820.2024.2335499

Lee, I., Ali, S., Zhang, H., DiPaola, D., & Breazeal, C. (2021, March). Developing middle school students' AI literacy. In J. F. Impagliazzo (Ed.), *Proceedings of the 52nd ACM Technical Symposium on Computer Science Education (SIGCSE '21)* (pp. 191–197). Association for Computing Machinery. https://doi.org/10.1145/3408877.3432413

Lin, P., & Van Brummelen, J. (2021, May). Engaging teachers to co-design integrated AI curriculum for K–12 classrooms. Y. Kitamura & A. Quigley (Eds.), *Proceedings of the 2021 CHI Conference on Human Factors in Computing Systems (CHI '21)* (pp. 1–12). Association for Computing Machinery. https://doi.org/10.1145/3411764.3445329

Long, D., & Magerko, B. (2020). What is AI literacy? In R. Bernhaupt (Ed.), *Proceedings of the 2020 CHI Conference on Human Factors in Computing Systems (CHI '20)* (pp. 1–13). Association for Computing Machinery. https://doi.org/10.1145/3313831.3376727

Ma, M., Ng, D. T. K., Liu, Z., & Wong, G. K. W. (2025). Fostering responsible AI literacy: A systematic review of K–12 AI ethics education. *Computers and Education: Artificial Intelligence, 8*, Article 100422. https://doi.org/10.1016/j.caeai.2025.100422

Miao, F., & Cukurova, M. (2024). *Artificial intelligence (AI) competency framework for teachers.* UNESCO. https://doi.org/10.54675/ZJTE2084

Miao, F., Shiohira, K., & Lao, N.. (2024). *Artificial intelligence (AI) competency framework for students.* UNESCO. https://doi.org/10.54675/JKJB9835

Mills, K., Ruiz, P., Lee, K.-W., Coenraad, M., Fusco, J., Roschelle, J., & Weisgrau, J. (2024). *AI literacy: A framework to understand, evaluate, and use emerging technology.* Digital Promise. https://doi.org/10.51388/20.500.12265/218

Ministry of Education and Higher Education, State of Qatar. (2018). *Computing and information technology curriculum for grades 10–12 (Qatar National Curriculum Framework).* https://cdn-files.abegs.org/abegs-marsad-prod/uploads/1d6e5f83-9a23-4d58-b9e8-d2c626bb6d0f.pdf

Ng, D. T. K., Su, J., Leung, J. K. L., & Chu, S. K. W. (2024). Artificial intelligence (AI) literacy education in secondary schools: A review. *Interactive Learning Environments, 32*(10), 6204–6224. https://doi.org/10.1080/10494820.2023.2255228

Organisation for Economic Co-operation and Development (OECD). (2019). OECD Learning Compass 2030. https://www.oecd.org/en/data/tools/oecd-learning-compass-2030.html

Organisation for Economic Co-operation and Development (OECD). (2025). *Empowering learners for the age of AI: AI literacy framework for primary and secondary education.* https://ailiteracyframework.org/

Schiff, D. (2022). Education for AI, not AI for education: The role of education and ethics in national AI policy strategies. *International Journal of Artificial Intelligence in Education, 32*(3), 527–563. https://doi.org/10.1007/s40593-021-00270-2

Sperling, K., Stenliden, L., Mannila, L., Hallstrom, J., Nordlof, C., & Heintz, F. (2025). Perspectives on AI literacy in middle school classrooms: An integrative review. *Postdigital Science Education, 7*(3), 719–749. https://doi.org/10.1007/s42438-025-00560-1

Touretzky, D. S., Gardner-McCune, C., Martin, F., & Seehorn, D. (2019, July). Envisioning AI for K–12: What should every child know about AI? In S. Kraus (Ed.), *Proceedings of the AAAI Conference on Artificial Intelligence* (Vol. 33, No. 1, pp. 9795–9799). AAAI Press. https://doi.org/10.1609/aaai.v33i01.33019795

Touretzky, D. S., Gardner-McCune, C., & Seehorn, D. (2023). Machine learning and the five big ideas in AI. *International Journal of Artificial Intelligence in Education, 33*(2), 233–266. https://doi.org/10.1007/s40593-022-00296-7

Viberg, O., Çukurova, M., Feldman-Maggor, Y., Alexandron, G., Shirai, S., Kanemune, S., Wasson, B., Tømte, C., Milrad, M., Coelho, R., & Kizilcec, R. F. (2025). What explains teachers' trust in AI in education across six countries? *Educational Technology Research and Development, 35*(3), 1288–1316. https://doi.org/10.1007/s40593-024-00433-x

Williams, R., Park, H. W., Oh, L., & Breazeal, C. (2019, July). PopBots: Designing an artificial intelligence curriculum for early childhood education. In S. Kraus (Ed.), *Proceedings of the AAAI Conference on Artificial Intelligence* (Vol. 33, No. 1, pp. 9729–9736). AAAI Press. https://doi.org/10.1609/aaai.v33i01.33019729

Yang, H., & Capan, S. (2025, April). *Promoting AI literacy in K–12: Components, challenges, and opportunities (CIGALE Expert Review Report).* SRI International. https://www.sri.com/wp-content/uploads/2025/04/CIGALE_ExpertReviewReport_Acc.pdf

Yang, Y., Zhang, Y., Sun, D., He, W., & Wei, Y. (2025). Navigating the landscape of AI literacy education: Insights from a decade of research (2014–2024). *Humanities and Social Sciences Communications, 12*, 374. https://doi.org/10.1057/s41599-025-04583-8

Yue, M., Jong, M.S.-Y., Dai, Y., & Lau, W.W.-F. (2025). Students as AI-literate designers: A pedagogical framework for learning and teaching AI literacy in elementary education. *Journal of Research on Technology in Education, 1–22*,. https://doi.org/10.1080/15391523.2025.2449942

Zhou, X., Li, Y., Chai, C. S., & Chiu, T. K. (2025). Defining, enhancing, and assessing artificial intelligence literacy and competency in K–12 education: A systematic review. *Interactive Learning Environments, 1–23*,. https://doi.org/10.1080/10494820.2025.2487538

Part II
Pedagogical Framework for AI Literacy in K–12 Education

This part establishes the theoretical and methodological blueprint for integrating AI literacy into teacher education. This part advances the discussion from the critical conceptual groundwork presented in Part I to the structured design, articulation, and validation of a pedagogical model. This model is explicitly designed to support educators in effectively translating AI literacy principles into K–12 classroom practice.

First, in Chap. 3, we introduce the Pedagogical Framework for AI Literacy, which responds to the pedagogical gap identified in the earlier chapters. This framework is grounded in three interconnected pillars—AI content knowledge, instructional process, and the learner development and identity—that together define what teachers should teach, how they can teach it, and how learners grow through the process. At its core is the Design–Create–Reflect (DCR) cycle, a pedagogical sequence that guides teachers and students through iterative design, ethical reasoning, and reflective inquiry. Chapter 3 details how these principles were synthesized into a coherent framework capable of supporting cross-disciplinary, developmentally appropriate integration of AI literacy in K–12 education.

Chapter 4 builds upon this conceptual design by focusing on rigorous validation. This chapter describes the systematic procedures undertaken to verify the framework's clarity, relevance, and theoretical soundness. Through structured expert review and systematic analysis, we outline how the framework's core components and instructional guidelines were refined and verified for consistency and pedagogical applicability in diverse teacher preparation contexts. The validation procedures confirm the framework's coherence as a guide for instructional planning, thereby providing the essential methodological foundation for the empirical comparative research presented in Part III.

Together, Chaps. 3 and 4 serve as the crucial bridge between conceptual exploration and empirical study. They document how a theoretically grounded framework is systematically developed into a validated, practical tool for preparing teachers to facilitate student learning, creation, and reflection in the age of intelligent technologies.

Chapter 3
Development of the Pedagogical Framework for AI Literacy

Abstract This chapter addresses the critical pedagogical deficit in K–12 AI literacy, detailing the development and design of a Pedagogical Framework for AI Literacy. The framework is built on three interconnected pillars to ensure systematic integration: AI content knowledge (based on the Five Big Ideas in AI), instructional process (guided by Human-Centered Design), and learner development and identity (informed by Science of Learning and Development principles). The framework's operational core is the Design-Create-Reflect (DCR) cycle. Each component of the DCR cycle synthesizes all three pillars into actionable teaching sequences that directly support educators. This design provides the explicit guidance necessary for teachers to integrate core AI concepts into existing disciplinary content without relying on specialized computer science instruction. Ultimately, the framework aims to provide the structure for equitable and sustainable AI literacy, shifting the focus from mere technical skills to fostering students' ethical reasoning and digital agency.

3.1 Introduction

In the preceding chapter, we established the multidimensional definition of AI literacy and confirmed the gaps in the literature related to the pedagogical deficit at the K–12 implementation level. Building directly on those findings, this chapter details the design and theoretical development of the Pedagogical Framework for AI Literacy. We move from abstract principles to actionable design, beginning by establishing the foundational vision and theoretical underpinnings of the framework, which is necessarily grounded in learning sciences, human-centered design, and ethical education principles. The framework is explicitly engineered to be modular and interdisciplinary, providing a coherent structure that supports educators in integrating AI concepts into subjects like history, literature, and mathematics, rather than treating AI as an add-on elective.

The core of this framework is the Design-Create-Reflect (DCR) cycle, a pedagogical cycle designed to enhance teacher capacity and student agency simultaneously. The subsequent sections of this chapter will detail the conceptual framing and

I. Lyublinskaya and X. Du, *A Pedagogical Framework for K–12 AI Literacy*, Springer Texts in Education, https://doi.org/10.1007/978-3-032-23570-1_3

vision setting that guided the framework's development, followed by the rigorous process of the initial framework design. We will then fully unpack the Design-Create-Reflect (DCR) cycle, presenting its structure, AI literacy competencies, and methods for fostering both ethical reflection and critical inquiry. This work culminates in presenting a tested, scalable tool intended to guide curriculum development, professional learning, and instructional practice, ensuring AI literacy becomes an integral pillar of K–12 education.

3.2 Conceptual Framing and Vision Setting

The first phase in developing the Pedagogical Framework for AI Literacy focused on establishing a solid conceptual foundation. This phase involved a systematic review of literature and practice-based insights to identify core needs in K–12 AI education and select the theoretical anchors that would shape the framework. The goal was to move beyond fragmented approaches to AI education and instead construct a comprehensive, developmentally appropriate, and equity-oriented vision.

The resulting framework is founded upon three distinct pillars, derived from researched models, which together provide the essential structure for our solution:

- AI content knowledge (the content anchor): This pillar sets the *what* of AI literacy expected of students and is defined by two interlocking components: the philosophical definition of AI literacy (the multidimensional model established in Chapter 2: Understand, Evaluate, and Use) and the instructional content. The core technical and social concepts that comprise the *instructional content* are organized using the Five Big Ideas in AI (Touretzky et al., 2019). This combination ensures the framework is both conceptually broad and practically structured for teaching foundational AI concepts.
- Instructional process (the process anchor): Focuses on the pedagogical approach necessary to support cross-disciplinary integration of AI literacy concepts. This pillar is explicitly grounded in design thinking and Human-Centered Design (HCD) models to ensure learning is iterative, contextually relevant, and focused on student-led creation.
- Learner development and identity (the disposition anchor): Guided by the principles of the Science of Learning and Development (SoLD) framework (Darling-Hammond et al., 2023), this pillar focuses on establishing a learning environment that supports the social and emotional needs of students, while actively promoting equity, confidence, and critical agency.

The subsequent sections detail the theoretical underpinnings of these three anchors, demonstrating how they combine to directly address the pedagogical deficit established in the preceding chapter.

3.2.1 AI Content Knowledge

Determining the core content students should learn is a critical first step in designing an effective pedagogical framework for AI literacy. There is growing recognition that K–12 students need structured, age-appropriate opportunities to understand not just how AI works, but also how it affects society. Our review focuses on the key efforts that have shaped this landscape, most notably the AI4K12 initiative, which defines the "Five Big Ideas in AI": Perception, Representation & Reasoning, Learning, Natural Interaction, and Social Impact. Developed through extensive consultation with educators, AI researchers, and learning scientists, the Five Big Ideas framework offers a scaffolded conceptual progression for introducing fundamental AI concepts from elementary through high school. Specifically, Touretzky et al., (2022) provide a detailed account of how these concepts can be aligned with national computer science standards and integrated into interdisciplinary learning experiences. However, the very technicality and structure of the Five Big Ideas offer a unique advantage for cross-curricular integration. Unlike broader frameworks, the specific descriptions of core concepts and learning progressions provide clear, definable intellectual anchors. This structured approach makes it easier for non-specialist teachers to identify concrete connections between AI principles (e.g., data and pattern recognition) and existing disciplinary practices (e.g., analyzing data in science or identifying patterns in mathematics). However, content definitions alone are insufficient without understanding how they are enacted in real-world classrooms. Druga et al. (2022) conducted a systematic review of 50 online AI education resources, using the TPACK (Technological Pedagogical Content Knowledge) framework to evaluate their effectiveness. Their findings highlight a critical shortcoming: while most resources support active engagement and hands-on experimentation, few incorporate all Five Big Ideas, and many lack scaffolded guidance, assessment tools, or teacher-friendly support. This underscores the need for a more holistic and coherent approach to AI content—one that goes beyond isolated activities to support full integration of AI literacy into the classroom context.

Equity is another pressing concern in AI education. Garg (2023) examined how the Five Big Ideas can be made accessible to underserved learners from low-income backgrounds, including non-English speakers with limited numeracy. Using a tinker-friendly tool to teach autoencoders, the study demonstrated that when designed thoughtfully, all five big ideas can be taught effectively to learners with significant educational barriers. The study also found increased curiosity and a stronger sense of agency among learners reinforcing the idea that AI content can empower students when it is made developmentally appropriate and inclusive. Together, these studies support our decision to adopt the Five Big Ideas in AI as the content anchor of our framework. The Big Ideas offer a rigorous yet flexible structure for organizing core AI concepts, while also aligning with contemporary pedagogical best practices and equity-oriented design. They serve as the foundation upon which competencies, learning outcomes, and activities can be meaningfully developed in K–12 settings.

3.2.2 Instructional Process

Effective AI literacy education must go beyond teaching abstract concepts and engage students in meaningful, hands-on learning that mirrors how AI is designed and used in the real world. To guide this pedagogical approach for cross-disciplinary integration, we anchor our Instructional Process pillar in Human-Centered Design (HCD; IDEO, 2015). HCD serves as the guiding philosophy because it intrinsically links problem-solving to user needs and empathy—critical elements for the Evaluate domain of AI literacy. HCD places empathy and human needs at the center of every stage, positioning students as designers who engage deeply with the needs of users and communities. This inherent focus on users and equity aligns closely with the ethical and civic goals of AI literacy. Furthermore, HCD aligns with constructivist learning theory, which posits that learners actively build knowledge through experiences, social interaction, and reflection rather than passively receiving information (Piaget, 1954; Vygotsky, 1978). Consistent with this theoretical foundation, HCD has been applied successfully in teacher education, particularly in preparing educators to guide students through ambiguity, foster creative problem-solving, and sustain reflective inquiry. It has also been shown to foster gender inclusivity and student engagement in STEM through interventions that build creative confidence and pro-social thinking (Kijima et al., 2021).

To implement this HCD philosophy, we adopt the design thinking model as the explicit, sequential instructional process (empathize, define, ideate, prototype, test). Design thinking has long been valued in education for enhancing problem-solving abilities, creativity, and student agency across project-based settings (Guaman-Quintanilla et al., 2023; Zulyusri et al., 2023). Furthermore, its iterative structure supports the development of critical thinking and collaborative inquiry (Bender-Salazar, 2023; Rösch et al., 2023). However, literature reveals significant limitations in its current K–12 application: a systematic review of design thinking integrated learning (DTIL) by Li and Zhan (2022) found that, despite being highly effective in theory, existing implementations often lack consistency in how core design practices are scaffolded and used. Moreover, most interventions focus narrowly on middle school STEM disciplines, often without long-term integration or equity-centered approaches.

This fragmentation, where the powerful potential of design thinking is undermined by inconsistent pedagogical application, confirms the lack of explicit scaffolding and pedagogical guidance noted throughout the literature review. Therefore, we adopt HCD as the theoretical foundation and the design thinking sequence as the structural blueprint, recognizing the need to refine this sequence into a more robust, developmentally appropriate, and inclusive methodology for cross-curricular integration of AI literacy.

3.2.3 Learner Development and Identity

A future-ready AI literacy framework must do more than convey technical skills or theoretical knowledge—it must nurture the full range of human capacities that enable young people to understand, question, and shape the technologies that impact their lives. Drawing upon this principle, we conducted a critical review of contemporary research that integrates the social, emotional, cognitive, and identity-related dimensions of learning. This review led us to adopt the Science of Learning and Development (SoLD; Darling-Hammond et al., 2023) as the Disposition Anchor of the framework. The SoLD framework is the result of decades of interdisciplinary research in neuroscience, developmental psychology, education, and learning sciences. It emphasizes that learning is not purely cognitive but is deeply shaped by students' social contexts, emotional states, cultural identities, and relationships with educators and peers.

Recent work by Darling-Hammond et al. (2023) synthesizes this body of knowledge to highlight the key capacities teachers must develop to nurture the whole child. These include fostering secure relationships, supporting identity formation, and creating rich, culturally responsive environments that empower students to thrive. Importantly, this research identifies not just what educators should know, but how teacher preparation must be structured to support deep, reflective, and adaptive professional learning. SoLD provides a foundation for reimagining educational experiences as identity-affirming, community-connected, and emotionally safe, where students feel seen and valued. García-Carrión (2023) extends this conversation by emphasizing the importance of co-creation and dialogic learning, especially in marginalized or under-resourced communities, ensuring learning environments are inclusive, culturally sustaining, and oriented toward long-term flourishing—not just academic achievement. In the context of AI literacy, this holistic view of development is essential. Students are not just future AI users or developers; they are decision-makers, citizens, and creators whose values, emotions, and identities influence how they engage with AI in society. Thus, the dispositional outcomes of an AI literacy framework—such as ethical awareness, digital agency, empathy, and responsible innovation—must be intentionally supported by research-informed design principles.

3.3 Initial Framework Design

The Initial Framework Design synthesized the three conceptual anchors defined in the preceding section (Content, Process, and Disposition) into a unified structure. The resulting Pedagogical Framework for AI Literacy is explicitly designed to guide the systematic integration of AI literacy into K–12 curricula across different disciplines. Its structure is built directly on the theoretical models chosen: the content anchor is defined by the Five Big Ideas in AI; the process anchor is guided by the HCD principles; and the disposition anchor is grounded in the SoLD framework. The purpose of this integrated structure is to support educators and curriculum developers in building students' understanding of AI while fostering the critical thinking, ethical reasoning, and design skills necessary for meaningful technological engagement.

The Five Big Ideas in AI define what students need to know to meaningfully engage with AI, e.g., how machines sense the world, process information, learn from data, interact with humans, and impact society. As a content anchor, these ideas provide a developmentally appropriate progression for building conceptual understanding across grade bands. They help educators scaffold lessons from basic awareness (e.g., how voice assistants work) to deeper critical engagement (e.g., how algorithms shape social decisions). HCD is adopted as the guiding philosophy for the pedagogical approach for cross-curricular integration of AI literacy because it intrinsically links problem-solving to user needs and empathy. To operationalize this philosophy, the framework utilizes the design thinking sequence (empathize, define, ideate, prototype, and test). This integrated design cycle empowers students not only to understand the mechanisms of AI, but to design with and around it in ways that respond to real-world needs. The process cultivates the skills and mindsets needed to design solutions using AI tools, evaluate outcomes, and adapt to new information while centering the human impact of technology. Furthermore, this approach supports equitable learning by inviting students to frame problems that matter to them and their communities. The SoLD framework serves as the theoretical guide for the disposition anchor. SoLD asserts that students' capacity to engage with complex technologies like AI is deeply shaped by their social, emotional, and cognitive growth, including their identity, relationships, and culturally responsive pedagogy. This holistic perspective is essential to foster the ethical awareness, collaborative skills, and growth mindset required for AI literacy. In this context, the SoLD framework informs how learning environments are structured to promote belonging, agency, and purpose, ensuring that students see themselves not as passive users of technology, but as capable, responsible, and reflective participants in shaping its future.

These three anchors are the interdependent pillars of the Pedagogical Framework for AI Literacy. This design ensures that when students explore AI concepts (content) through hands-on, human-centered challenges (process), in environments that promote identity and equity (disposition), the result is a dynamic learning experience that blends technical understanding, creative application, and human values. The pedagogical framework thus provides the holistic structure necessary to avoid reducing AI literacy to a checklist of competencies. To guide the teacher in integrating AI literacy across disciplines, we propose a core pedagogical cycle, the Design–Create–Reflect (DCR) cycle. This model represents the functional structure of the Pedagogical Framework for AI Literacy, drawing on the iterative, human-centered structure of HCD and the developmental insights of SoLD.

3.4 Design-Create-Reflect (DCR) Cycle

The third phase of the development of the Pedagogical Framework for AI Literacy involved the design of the DCR cycle, a three-component pedagogical structure that synthesizes the framework's three pillars into an actionable teaching sequence. The DCR cycle embodies the philosophical principles of HCD and SoLD while guiding the integration of the Five Big Ideas into cross-disciplinary lessons.

3.4.1 Design Component

The Design component is the first stage of the DCR cycle that serves as the investigative stage of the pedagogical framework. This component was developed by synthesizing the framework's content anchor with the principles of the process and disposition anchors. This component is rooted in the HCD philosophy, which guides its overall ethical purpose. To operationalize this HCD philosophy, the design component utilizes the initial stages of the design thinking process, specifically focusing on empathize, define, and ideate steps. In this stage, the teacher is guided to create learning experiences where students engage in contextual analysis to surface real-world user needs and ethical tensions related to a disciplinary topic. These activities are designed to support students in identifying design opportunities and reframing problems in ways that are socially grounded and equity-oriented. In doing so, students cultivate empathy not as a passive trait but as an active research stance that guides responsible inquiry and design.

The AI content knowledge (Five Big Ideas) is intentionally woven into this component by helping students recognize how core AI concepts manifest in real-world systems during the empathize, define, and ideate steps of the design thinking process. For instance, a mathematics teacher might introduce the context of image recognition as middle school students study measures of central tendency. Students would then explore how a computer processes data structures (Representation and Reasoning) to make decisions about images, examining how different data points (Perception) interact to influence the classification output (Lyublinskaya & Du, 2025).

Furthermore, SoLD emphasizes that deep learning and honest investigation require students to feel seen, safe, and connected to the purpose of their work. The teacher is guided to establish a safe and inclusive environment essential for the Design component's early stages, allowing students to freely discuss, challenge, and explore sensitive user problems relevant to their disciplinary content. This means teachers create spaces where students can openly frame and investigate issues through the lenses of identity and fairness, supporting the development of student agency as they learn to question and influence the design of solutions in their community.

The instructional outcomes for the Design component are defined by two core AI literacy competencies. These competencies are not arbitrary; rather, they emerge from the synergistic relationship between the three foundational pillars. The Process

(HCD) dictates the structure of inquiry, the Content (5BIs) provides the conceptual focus, and the Disposition (SoLD) ensures the process is grounded in equitable, human-centered values. This combined approach yields the following core competencies for the Design component:

- D1. Problem framing and idea generation: Students demonstrate proficiency in the initial design process, including empathetic understanding needs, defining authentic problems, and generating innovative ideas for solutions.
- D2. Critically evaluating AI applications: Students critically evaluate AI technologies, including assessing their effectiveness, accuracy, perspective, and credibility in various applications and contexts.

3.4.2 Create Component

Following the problem-framing and contextual inquiry of the Design component, the Create component guides the teacher in designing experiences where students translate their ideas into tangible prototypes, models, or systems. This component reflects core principles of constructionist learning theory, emphasizing that understanding is deepened through the design and manipulation of artifacts that are personally meaningful and socially relevant.

The teacher is guided to organize activities that leverage the prototype and test stages of the design thinking process. This approach is rooted in project-based learning and design-based inquiry, mirroring the iterative nature of professional computational modeling. The teacher designs testing cycles and structures peer feedback opportunities where students engage in practical work. The focus of these experiences is to integrate core AI concepts derived from the Five Big Ideas (content anchor), such as algorithmic logic, abstraction, and natural language processing into domain-specific disciplinary topics. For instance, an elementary school teacher in a lesson about people migration can have students create interactive maps of immigrants' journeys supported by short stories. Students could then use their stories as prompts for the chatbot to become a story teller and explore concepts of natural interaction and data bias. (Lyublinskaya & Du, 2025). Through these design choices, the teacher ensures learners explore trade-offs between model accuracy and fairness, test edge cases, and consider the implications of their design decisions, thereby integrating technical understanding with ethical reasoning within the creation process. Moreover, the Create component encourages collaboration and co-design, where students build and test their systems in dialogue with peers and, where possible, with the communities they seek to serve. Students not only refine their own prototypes but learn to give and receive constructive feedback developing a sense of collective responsibility for the impact of the tools they are designing.

The Create component also emphasizes the agency of learners as designers—not simply as users or critics of AI, but as creators who can shape systems with intention and care. This builds on work in maker learning and digital fabrication, which highlights how building functional prototypes promotes engagement, persistence, and critical thinking. Importantly, the focus is not on coding proficiency alone but on how computational thinking concepts—such as algorithmic logic, abstraction, and pattern recognition—can be applied in socially grounded ways.

To define the instructional outcomes for this component, two AI literacy competencies were derived. These competencies emerge directly from the synergistic interaction between the Content, Process, and Disposition anchors within the Create component's structure, ensuring that the teacher's designed experience fosters both technical application and ethical responsibility:

- C1. Prototyping and iterative testing of solutions: Students transform ideas into tangible prototypes, systematically testing them against criteria. They analyze results, extract essential information, and iterate on solutions for improvement.
- C2. Collaborative design and ethical responsibility: Students engage in co-design and peer review, leveraging collaborative skills and ethical principles to evaluate the fairness, social relevance, and human impact of their system, thereby demonstrating collective responsibility.

3.4.3 Reflect Component

The Reflect component guides the teacher in designing learning experiences that invite students to critically examine the broader social, emotional, and ethical dimensions of the AI systems they have studied or created. Designed to avoid treating reflection as a final or isolated activity, this component mandates a recursive and integrative approach, guiding the teacher to structure activities that encourage students to revisit their assumptions, design choices, and the societal impact of their work. Rooted in traditions of critical pedagogy, moral development, and the SoLD principles, the Reflect component provides the instructional structure necessary to support students in making meaning of their experiences while developing a stronger sense of identity, agency, and purpose.

The SoLD framework plays a central role in shaping the Reflect component by emphasizing that deep, transferable learning emerges when students feel a sense of belonging and can connect their work to personal values and lived experiences. The component is designed to ensure reflection is not abstract or theoretical, but rather grounded in students' disciplinary work and their engagement with complex issues. This grounding guides the teacher to structure the environment so students are empowered to critically examine how AI systems intersect with questions of fairness, privacy, equity, and power. By ensuring this safe space, the teacher facilitates the final, high-stakes reflection necessary for students to formulate their own roles in shaping a more just technological future within the context of their specific disciplinary knowledge.

This component also draws on the Five Big Ideas in AI, particularly Societal Impact, as a conceptual anchor for reflection. The teacher is provided with tools to guide students in analyzing the ripple effects of AI systems—Who benefits? Who is harmed? What values are embedded in the algorithms? For instance, to facilitate this ethical inquiry, in a high school biology lesson about natural genetic variations, the teacher could also include debates about ethical implications of using AI to influence genetic variations through AI-augmented selective breeding or AI-assisted gene editing (Lyublinskaya & Du, 2025). This framing pushes learners beyond technical evaluation to consider the civic implications of their work within that disciplinary context. The framework also recommends and supports the integration of specific instructional tools—such as ethical dilemma case studies, stakeholder audits, positionality mapping, and journaling—to foster critical inquiry and deeper metacognitive awareness.

From a HCD perspective, the Reflect component aligns with the core principle of iteration informed by not just technical, but social and ethical feedback as well. This alignment guides the teacher to structure reflection activities where students consider how their solutions are perceived by others, how well they address the needs of users, and whether their intentions align with outcomes. This invites a level of humility and openness that is essential for developing ethical judgment in complex, real-world settings.

As the final component of the DCR cycle, the Reflect component requires a synthesis of learning, where the competencies are derived by connecting the Content, Process, and Disposition anchors ensuring that the teacher's designed experience fosters deep review and future orientation:

- R1. Metacognitive and ethical self-assessment: Students reflect on the entire DCR process, evaluating the success, ethical trade-offs, and unforeseen societal impacts of their solutions, and articulating how design choices and data bias influenced the outcome.
- R2. Informing future design and digital agency: Students propose actionable revisions to their solutions, formulate principles for responsible innovation, and communicate their final findings to stakeholders, thereby demonstrating digital agency.

3.5 Conclusion

To conclude, we present our final Pedagogical Framework for AI Literacy. It is grounded in the established theoretical anchors, Human-Centered Design (HCD), the Five Big Ideas in AI, and the Science of Learning and Development (SoLD), and utilizes the Design-Create-Reflect (DCR) cycle as its core instructional cycle. This framework addresses the critical pedagogical deficit identified in Chapter 2 by providing a coherent structure for AI literacy integration across K-12 curriculum. This framework is constructed as a practical pedagogical tool to support educators in building students' competencies, ensuring they can navigate and shape an AI-driven world. A corresponding visual representation further illustrates the cyclical and interconnected nature of the framework, emphasizing the iterative process of designing, creating, and reflecting within real-world contexts (Fig. 3.1).

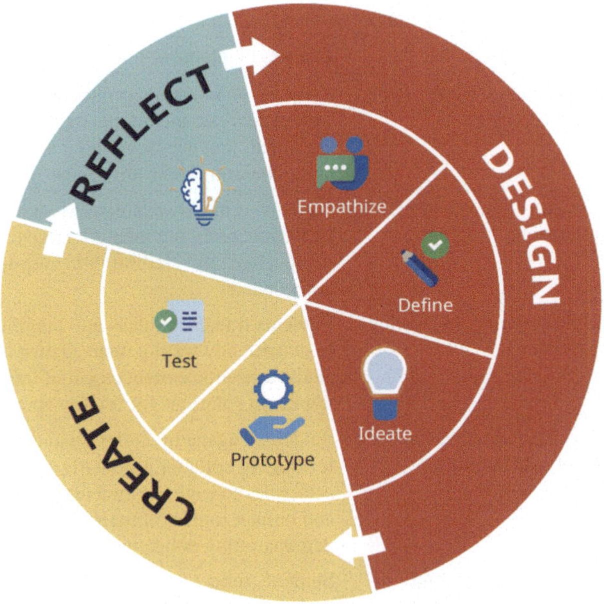

Fig. 3.1 The Design-Create-Reflect (DCR) pedagogical cycle. Reprinted from *Teaching AI Literacy Across the Curriculum. A K-12 Handbook* (p. 34) by I. Lyublinskaya & X. Du, 2025, Corwin. Reprinted with permission

Table 3.1 outlines the key components of the framework, specifying associated competencies, and intended learning outcomes, thereby providing teachers with a clear structural guide for lesson design and assessment.

Table 3.1 Summary of DCR cycle components and associated AI literacy competencies

Component	Competencies	Learning Outcomes
DESIGN	D1. Problem framing and idea generation	Students demonstrate proficiency in the initial design process, including empathetic understanding needs, defining authentic problems, and generating innovative ideas for solutions
	D2. Critically evaluating AI applications	Students critically evaluate AI technologies, including assessing their effectiveness, accuracy, perspective, and credibility in various applications and contexts
CREATE	C1. Prototyping and testing solutions	Students transform ideas into tangible prototypes, systematically testing them against criteria. They analyze results, extract essential information, and iterate on solutions for improvement
	C2. Collaborative design and ethical responsibility	Students engage in co-design and peer review, leveraging collaborative skills and ethical principles to evaluate the fairness, social relevance, and human impact of their system, thereby demonstrating collective responsibility
REFLECT	R1. Metacognitive and ethical self-assessment	Students reflect on the entire DCR process, evaluating the success, ethical trade-offs, and unforeseen societal impacts of their solutions, and articulating how design choices and data bias influenced the outcome
	R2. Informing future design and digital agency	Students propose actionable revisions to their solutions, formulate principles for responsible innovation, and communicate their final findings to stakeholders, thereby demonstrating digital agency

References

Bender-Salazar, R. (2023). Design thinking as an effective method for problem-setting and needfinding for entrepreneurial teams addressing wicked problems. *Journal of Innovation and Entrepreneurship, 12*(1), 24. https://doi.org/10.1186/s13731-023-00291-2

Darling-Hammond, L., Schachner, A., Wojcikiewicz, S. K., & Flook, L. (2023). Educating teachers to enact the science of learning and development. *Applied Developmental Science, 27*(2), 73–89. https://doi.org/10.1080/10888691.2022.2130506

Druga, S., Otero, N., & Ko, A. J. (2022, July). The landscape of teaching resources for AI education. In E. Barendsen & Simon (Eds.), *Proceedings of the 27th ACM conference on innovation and technology in computer science education* (Vol. 1, pp. 96–102). https://dl.acm.org/doi/abs/ https://doi.org/10.1145/3502718.3524782

Garg, S., (2023). Democratising AI education: Teaching autoencoders to out-of-school children from low-income backgrounds. In C. K. Looi, M. Chang, & M. Yoshida (Eds.) *Proceedings of the international conference on computers in education* (pp. 861–866). https://doi.org/10.58459/icce.2023.1148

García-Carrión, R. (2023). The science of learning and development: A commentary. *Review of Research in Education, 47*(1), 155–160. https://doi.org/10.3102/0091732X231218731

Guaman-Quintanilla, S., Everaert, P., Chiluiza, K., & Valcke, M. (2023). Impact of design thinking in higher education: A multi-actor perspective on problem solving and creativity. *International*

Journal of Technology and Design Education, 33(1), 217–240. https://doi.org/10.1007/s10798-021-09724-z

IDEO (2015) *The field guide to human-centered design.* https://www.designkit.org/.

Kijima, R., Yang-Yoshihara, M., & Maekawa, M. S. (2021). Using design thinking to cultivate the next generation of female STEAM thinkers. *International Journal of STEM Education, 8*(1), 14. https://doi.org/10.1186/s40594-021-00271-6

Lee, C. D., Lerner, R. M., Gadsden, V. L., & Osher, D. (2023). The science of learning and development: A view of the issues. *Review of Research in Education, 47*(1), ix-xviii. https://doi.org/10.3102/0091732X24124474

Li, T., & Zhan, Z. (2022). A systematic review on design thinking integrated learning in K-12 education. *Applied Sciences, 12*(7), 3457. https://doi.org/10.3390/app12168077

Lyublinskaya, I., & Du, X. (2025). *Teaching AI literacy across the curriculum. A K-12 handbook.* Corwin.

Piaget, J. (1954). *The construction of reality in the child.* Basic Books.

Rösch, N., Tiberius, V., & Kraus, S. (2023). Design thinking for innovation: Context factors, process, and outcomes. *European Journal of Innovation Management, 26*(7), 160–176. https://doi.org/10.1108/EJIM-03-2022-0164

Touretzky, D. S., Gardner-McCune, C., Martin, F., & Seehorn, D. (2019, July). Envisioning AI for K–12: What should every child know about AI? In S. Kraus (Ed.), *Proceedings of the AAAI conference on artificial intelligence* (Vol. 33, No. 1, pp. 9795–9799). AAAI Press. https://doi.org/10.1609/aaai.v33i01.33019795

Touretzky, D., Gardner-McCune, C., & Seehorn, D. (2022). Machine learning and the five big ideas in AI. *International Journal of Artificial Intelligence in Education, 32*(1), 82–94. https://doi.org/10.1007/s40593-022-00314-1

Vygotsky, L. S. (1978). *Mind in society: The development of higher psychological processes.* Harvard University Press.

Zulyusri, Z., Santosa, T. A., Festiyed, F., Yerimadesi, Y., Yohandri, Y., Razak, A., & Sofianora, A. (2023). Effectiveness of STEM learning based on design thinking in improving critical thinking skills in science learning: A meta-analysis. *Journal Penelitian Pendidikan IPA, 9*(2), 234–247. https://doi.org/10.29303/jppipa.v9i6.3709

Chapter 4
Validation of the Pedagogical Framework for AI Literacy

Abstract This chapter describes the validation process of the pedagogical framework, specifically, the theoretical DCR cycle designed to guide K-12 teacher preparation for AI literacy integration. The validation employed a multi-faceted approach utilizing data from 164 preservice teacher lesson plans and expert review. Content validity was established through an iterative review by a panel of subject matter experts (SMEs), resulting in the substantive revision of three core AI literacy competencies to eliminate conceptual overlap and ambiguity. Inter-rater reliability of the coding scheme was achieved through a structured debriefing process that resolved initial inconsistencies arising from the Base Rate Problem. Construct validity was tested by comparing the hypothesized 3-factor structure against the 1-factor model. The theoretical model was rejected due to statistical non-admissibility. The single-factor model achieved an excellent fit and was confirmed as the only statistically viable structure. This finding was independently supported by parallel analysis and scree plot examination. The convergence of evidence confirms that while the DCR cycle remains the pedagogical guide for instruction, the six competencies empirically coalesce into a single, reliable scale: Overall AI Literacy competence. This validated, unified structure provides the foundation for the comparative studies in subsequent chapters.

4.1 Introduction

In the preceding chapter, we detailed the development of the Pedagogical Framework for AI Literacy, centered on the Design-Create-Reflect (DCR) cycle. This framework was built upon a synthesis of AI content knowledge, human-centered design principles, and learning science, establishing a theoretical model designed to guide K-12 teachers to integrate AI literacy across the curriculum. The primary purpose of this chapter is to confirm the validity of the DCR cycle. First, content validity was tested by soliciting and incorporating detailed expert feedback on the relevance and clarity of the competencies, which resulted in the substantive revision of three out of six core competencies. Second, we tested the construct validity by

I. Lyublinskaya and X. Du, *A Pedagogical Framework for K–12 AI Literacy*, Springer Texts in Education, https://doi.org/10.1007/978-3-032-23570-1_4

assessing the internal consistency reliability of the three hypothesized DCR components and providing theoretical justification for their distinction. To do that, we used the Kuder-Richardson Formula 20 on the binary data gathered from the 164 lesson plans developed by our preservice teacher cohorts. This analysis provides the empirical evidence necessary to determine which components of the DCR cycle can be reliably measured as cohesive, distinct scales in the subsequent cross-cultural comparison.

4.2 Content Validation

In order to establish that the AI literacy competencies (D1, D2, C1, C2, R1, R2) identified in the DCR cycle are relevant, comprehensive, and clearly articulated from a pedagogical and domain expertise standpoint, we engaged a panel of three Subject Matter Experts (SMEs). These SMEs were carefully chosen based on their deep experience at the intersection of AI, curriculum development, and K-12 education. The small size of the panel facilitated a rigorous, high-fidelity review process. The panel comprised:

- SME1: AI and STEM education faculty with an interdisciplinary background across mathematics, computer science, and education, bringing extensive teaching and leadership experience from both K-12 schools and higher education. Their research expertise spans AI in education, STEM/Mathematics education, educational policy, and teacher education, with a current emphasis on AI-enhanced learning, teaching, and digital well-being.
- SME2: AI and analytics in education faculty with expertise in the theoretical and practical application of AI, focusing on intelligent support in exploratory and open-ended learning environments, educational data mining, and learning analytics. Their research background in STEM and educational technology ensured a strong methodological perspective on operationalizing the framework's components.
- SME3: School District Curriculum Specialist. A highly experienced teacher now at a district level, with extensive experience in curriculum development and technology integration across multiple schools. This perspective offered critical practical feedback on the feasibility, clarity, and system-level utility of the competencies.

The review procedure provided the SMEs with the DCR framework and open-ended questions designed to solicit detailed qualitative feedback on three primary areas: relevance (Are these the correct AI literacy competencies?), completeness (Is anything missing?), and clarity (Are the definitions operational?). The evaluations were conducted independently.

The independent expert reviews confirmed the high relevance of the DCR competencies but identified critical areas of conceptual overlap and ambiguity that required substantive revision. This qualitative feedback generally supported the three-factor

Table 4.1 Summary of revisions to AI literacy competencies based on SMEs' feedback

Original competencies	SMEs' feedback	Revised competencies
C2. Applying AI to solve real-world problems	C2 contains the specific activities listed in C1, refocus C2 on disposition and social outcome, while leaving technical aspects to C1	C2. Collaborative design and ethical responsibility
R1. Developing ethical awareness in AI	Significant overlap with D2, refocus R1 on metacognition and self-assessment related to ethical AI	R1. Metacognitive and ethical self-assessment
R2. Responsible use of AI technologies with real-world application for the community through collaboration	Significant overlap with C2, refocus R2 on agency, lifelong learning, or advocacy	R2. Informing future design and digital agency

structure (DCR) but mandated a clearer delineation between certain indicators, particularly within the Create (C) and Reflect (R) components. The table 4.1 summarizes the key feedback and the resulting substantive changes to three of the six core competencies.

These revisions significantly enhanced the structural fidelity of the DCR framework, ensuring that the six final competencies were conceptually clean. This expert consensus on the refined framework provides the necessary evidence of its content validity before proceeding to the empirical construct validation.

4.3 Construct Validation

The construct validation process involved a sequence of methodological steps to empirically test the framework's internal structure. First, we developed the Planning AI Literacy Integration template consistent with the DCR cycle. The template was used by the preservice teachers to develop lesson plans that integrated AI literacy into the standards-based curriculum. The lesson plans were collected and coded for the evidence of competencies prioritized by the preservice teachers. Finally, we used these binary data to test the internal consistency reliability of the three DCR components using the Kuder-Richardson Formula 20 (KR-20) statistic.

4.3.1 The Planning AI Literacy Integration Template

The Planning AI Literacy Integration template was modified from the Understanding by Design (UbD) framework (Wiggins & McTighe, 2005) to align discipline-specific learning outcomes with the identified AI literacy learning objectives and outcomes.

This modification ensures that the development of AI literacy is treated not as an add-on, but as an integral part of the standards-based curriculum. The template functions as a three-stage design tool, guiding educators to plan instruction with the end goals in mind, and ensuring alignment between discipline-specific learning outcomes and the identified AI literacy objectives. (Lyublinskaya & Du, 2025).

The three stages of the template are structured as follows:

- Stage 1: Desired results. This stage focuses on long-term goals and foundational understanding. Prompts guide the teacher to define instructional goals, essential questions, and core understandings for both the subject-specific content and the corresponding AI literacy competencies.
- Stage 2: Assessment evidence. This stage focuses on planning backward from desired results. It requires the teacher to define evaluative criteria and design performance tasks that explicitly require students to demonstrate both their subject-specific knowledge and their attainment of AI literacy outcomes.
- Stage 3: Learning plan. This stage is where the DCR cycle is embedded. Instead of a traditional lesson plan, this stage is structured around the steps of the design thinking process, which aligns directly with the Design-Create-Reflect (DCR) cycle. Within this stage, prompts guide the teachers to link activities to the framework.

This intentional alignment across the three UbD stages and the embedding of the DCR cycle within Stage 3 ensured that every lesson plan collected provided the explicit data required to score the presence or absence of each of the six binary indicators.

4.3.2 Data Preparation and Inter-Rater Reliability

The data originated from the 164 completed lesson planning templates developed by the preservice teacher cohorts. Each template was coded using six AI literacy competencies (D1, D2, C1, C2, R1, R2). Specifically, a researcher reviewed each lesson plan and coded the presence or absence of a specific competency's requirement to define the score. Score 1 (present) was assigned if the lesson plan provided clear and explicit evidence that the teacher intended to develop the competency (e.g., if the lesson plan included an activity satisfying R1). Score 0 (absent) was assigned if the lesson plan activity was absent, implied, or did not meet the defined criteria for that specific competency. This resulted in a binary dataset where each lesson plan yielded six scores (0 or 1), one for each indicator.

To ensure the inter-rater reliability of the coding process, a second independent coder applied the scoring protocol to a random sample of 30 lesson plans, comprising 18.3% of the sample. We chose to prioritize consistency of application and reported the raw percent agreement alongside Cohen's Kappa statistic (Cohen, 1960) since the Cohen's Kappa statistic that is typically utilized to assess agreement for categorical data (Cohen, 1960) is known to be overly sensitive to the prevalence of agreement

Table 4.2 Percent agreement for inter-rater reliability

Competency	Initial agreement	Cohen's κ	Final agreement	Cohen's κ
D1 (Problem framing and idea generation)	24/30 (80%)	.207	28/30 (93.3%)	.793
D2 (Critically evaluating AI applications)	24/30 (80%)	.302	30/30 (100%)	1.00
C1 (Prototyping and testing solutions)	30/30 (100%)	.000	30/30 (100%)	1.00
C2 (Collaborative design and ethical responsibility)	22/30 (73.3%)	-.143	28/30 (93.3%)	.862
R1 (Metacognitive and ethical self-assessment)	22/30 (73.3%)	.333	29/30 (96.7%)	.927
R2 (Informing future design and digital agency)	15/30 (50%)	-.190	29/30 (96.7%)	.783

in the data. When categories are heavily imbalanced, or when one score is highly prevalent (a known Base Rate Problem), Kappa can be biased and may not accurately reflect true consensus (Li et al., 2023). The initial analysis, however, revealed that even though raw percent agreement was acceptable for some indicators (e.g., D1, D2, and C1), the kappa values were low or negative (Table 4.2). This poor statistical result, particularly for C2, R1, and R2, signaled significant ambiguity and need for clarification of the learning outcomes.

Consequently, the coders engaged in a focused debriefing to analyze disagreement patterns and collaboratively clarify the criteria for these problematic learning outcomes. The clarification notes for each learning outcome defined specific criteria for coding each competency (Table 4.3).

The lesson plans were then coded again using the clarification notes. The final analysis confirmed that the iterative refinement process was highly successful, establishing the reliability of the full dataset (Table 4.2) The calculated Cohen's κ values, ranging from .783 to 1.00, confirm substantial to perfect agreement for all six competencies. This consistently high level of inter-rater agreement demonstrates the objectivity of the coding scheme and confirms that the results are not dependent on the individual coders, thus ensuring measurement reliability for the full dataset.

4.3.3 Empirical Structure Validation

To achieve construct validity, we employed a multi-phased approach to determine the empirical dimensionality of the DCR framework. Consistent with the recommended practice for structural equation modeling (Anderson & Gerbing, 1988), we assessed the adequacy of the proposed theoretical structure by explicitly comparing

Table 4.3 Clarification notes for AI literacy competencies

Competencies	Clarification notes
D1. Problem framing and idea generation	The problem must be authentically defined or significantly reframed by the student, not just posed by the teacher
D2. Critically evaluating AI applications	Requires students to evaluate the effectiveness, accuracy, bias, or credibility of the AI tool or the data it uses
C1. Prototyping and testing solutions	Students must create a product as a solution to the problem they defined
C2. Collaborative design and ethical responsibility	Besides collaborative design, there must be an explicit discussion on ethical principles, fairness, social relevance, or human impact of the solution
R1. Metacognitive and ethical self-assessment	Reflection must be on the whole DCR process including ethical trade-offs or societal impacts, not just on the subject matter
R2. Informing future design and digital agency	Requires students to propose revisions, discuss future applications, or communicate their final findings (reports, presentations) to an audience

the hypothesized three-factor model (DCR) against the most parsimonious alternative, the single-factor model. This comparative confirmatory factor analysis (CFA) was conducted using AMOS 30 on a full dataset. The requirements of sample sizes for conducting a CFA are inconsistent across studies, so we used a ratio-based rule of at least 10 data points for every variable in the model (Gagné & Hancock, 2006). Based on this criterion, the sample size ($N = 164$) was sufficient to evaluate the structure of the DCR cycle. The results of CFA strongly support the one-factor model (Table 4.4).

The theoretical three-factor model was rejected because it failed to achieve an admissible solution, rendering its fit metrics unreliable. In contrast, the single-factor model achieved an excellent fit. Both, comparative fit index (CFI) and Tucker-Lewis index (TLI) were above the accepted value of 0.9 (Bentler, 1990). The ratio $\chi^2/df < 3.0$ indicated a good fit (Kline, 2005) and the root mean square error for approximation

Table 4.4 Comparison of CFA results for 1-factor and 3-factor models

Fit index	3-factor model (DCR)	1-factor model (overall AI literacy)
Chi-squared	$\chi^2(6) = 8.510$ ($p = .203$)	$\chi^2(9) = 9.381$ ($p = .403$)
χ^2/df	1.42 < 3.0	1.04 < 3.0
CFI	.980 > .9	.997 > .9
TLI	.950 > .9	.995 > .9
RMSEA	.051 > .05	.016 < .05
Iteration limit	The iteration limit was reached before a local minimum was found	Minimum was achieved
Admissibility	Rejected	Accepted

Table 4.5 Comparison of eigenvalues in PCA and PA

Factor	Eigenvalues	
	PCA	PA
1	2.106	1.356
2	1.153	1.196
3	.984	1.097
4	.785	1.009
5	.597	0.922
6	.376	0.835

(RMSEA) was smaller than the preferred value of 0.05 (Fabrigar, 1999). Thus, CFA confirmed the single-factor model as the only admissible structural model.

To provide definitive, independent confirmation that the six competencies represent only one factor, we completed two data-driven tests: parallel analysis (PA) and scree plot analysis using SPSS 30. For PA, the eigenvalues from the actual data were compared against the 95th percentile eigenvalues derived from 1,000 randomly generated datasets ($N = 164$, Nvars = 6). The PA demonstrated that only the first factor's eigenvalue exceeded the random data baseline, confirming that only one factor should be retained (Hayton et al., 2004). Thus, PA confirmed one-factor model for AI literacy competency (Table 4.5).

Finally, the visual inspection of the scree plot obtained from the initial Principal Components Analysis (PCA) completed in SPSS 30 showed a clear and pronounced "elbow" at the second factor, confirming the strong variance explained by the single first factor and supporting the conclusion of the PA. (Fig. 4.1).

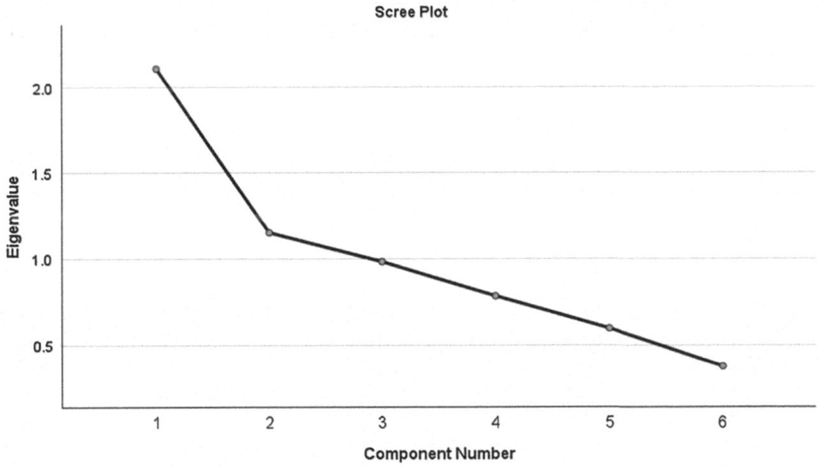

Fig. 4.1 PCA scree plot suggesting one-factor model

This convergence of statistical evidence—the superior fit of the CFA, the decisive result of PA, and the visual confirmation from the Scree Plot—demonstrates that the six DCR competencies function as reliable indicators of one single, unified construct.

4.4 Conclusion

This chapter accomplished the critical task of validating the Pedagogical Framework for AI Literacy, providing the necessary empirical foundation for the comparative studies in Part III. The validation was achieved through a comprehensive, multi-faceted process:

1. Content validity: Confirmed through the iterative expert review, resulting in the substantive revision of three core competencies (C2, R1, and R2) and the establishment of clear operational clarification notes, ensuring the framework's pedagogical relevance.
2. Inter-rater reliability: Established through an iterative inter-rater process that achieved substantial to perfect final Cohen's Kappa values ($\kappa \geq 0.783$) across all six competencies, confirming the objectivity and trustworthiness of the data coding.
3. Construct validation: Achieved through rigorous model comparison (CFA) and data-driven methods (PA and scree plot). The evidence converged to reject the hypothesized multidimensional structure.

The statistical evidence confirms that the six AI literacy competencies, as coded in the lesson plans developed by preservice teachers, coalesce into a single, unified construct. The DCR cycle is retained as the pedagogical process essential for guiding teachers' planning sequences, which aligns with the backward design principles of the UbD template. However, the final validated model is a single-factor structure representing overall AI literacy competency, which achieved an excellent and highly parsimonious fit and was the only statistically viable solution.

References

Anderson, J. C., & Gerbing, D. W. (1988). Structural equation modeling in practice: A review and recommended two-step approach. *Psychological Bulletin, 103*(3), 411–423. https://doi.org/10.1037/0033-2909.103.3.411

Bentler, P. (1990). Comparative fit indexes in structural models. *Psychological Bulletin, 107*(2), 238–246. https://doi.org/10.1037/0033-2909.107.2.238

Cohen, J. (1960). A coefficient of agreement for nominal scales. *Educational and Psychological Measurement, 20*(1), 37–46. https://doi.org/10.1177/001316446002000104

Fabrigar, L., Wegener, D., MacCallum, R., & Strahan, E. (1999). Evaluating the use of exploratory factor analysis in psychological research. *Psychological Methods, 4*(3), 272–299. https://doi.org/10.1037/1082-989X.4.3.272

Gagné, P., & Hancock, G. R. (2006). Measurement model quality, sample size, and solution propriety in confirmatory factor models. *Multivariate Behavioral Research, 41*(1), 65–83. https://doi.org/10.1207/s15327906mbr4101_5

Hayton, J. C., Allen, D. G., & Scarpello, V. (2004). Factor retention decisions in Exploratory Factor Analysis: A tutorial on parallel analysis. *Organizational Research Methods, 7*, 191–205. https://doi.org/10.1177/1094428104263675

Kline, R. (2005) *Principles and practices of structural equation modeling* (2nd ed.). Guilford.

Li, M., Gao, Q., & Yu, T. (2023). Kappa statistical considerations in evaluating inter-rater reliability between two raters: Which, when and context matters. *BMC Cancer, 23*(1), 799. https://doi.org/10.1186/s12885-023-11325-z

Lyublinskaya, I., & Du, X. (2025) *Teaching AI literacy across the curriculum. A K-12 handbook.* Corwin.

Wiggins, G., & McTighe, J. (2005). *Understanding by design* (Expanded 2nd ed.). Association for Supervision and Curriculum Development.

Part III
Empirical Studies on Teacher Competency and AI Literacy Integration: A US—China Comparative Study

This part contains the core empirical investigations of this book. It presents a comprehensive, cross-cultural study exploring the effectiveness of a targeted course intervention designed to prepare preservice teachers to apply the Pedagogical Framework for AI Literacy (developed and validated in Part II). This part analyzes the complete process, from developing the teachers' foundational AI literacy to assessing their capability to translate that knowledge into instructional practice in two distinct national contexts.

The inquiry begins in Chap. 5 by detailing the research design and contextual factors. This chapter outlines the architecture of the intervention course, AI Literacy for Educators, which serves as the foundation for the subsequent empirical studies. Chapter 5 describes the pedagogical approach, the curriculum's alignment with the framework, and the characteristics of the participants: preservice teachers from both the United States and China. This chapter establishes the rigorous context for a comprehensive inquiry into how a single pedagogical intervention can influence content knowledge, ethical awareness, and instructional design practices in two distinct national contexts.

Next, we shift to quantitative and qualitative investigations of impact:

- Chapter 6 investigates the direct impact of the course on participants' AI Content Knowledge. This study measures changes in their knowledge and skills related to the *Five Big Ideas in AI* (Perception, Representation & Reasoning, Learning, Natural Interaction, and Societal Impact). By comparing data from Chinese and American participants, the chapter highlights how cultural and contextual factors may influence the development of these core competencies.
- Chapter 7 builds on this foundation by exploring preservice teachers' ethical awareness and critical reflection regarding AI. The chapter assesses how the course shapes participants' critical reflection on issues like fairness, transparency, and accountability. It applies the same comparative lens as Chapter 6 to identify similar or divergent patterns in ethical reasoning between the Chinese and American cohorts.

- Chapter 8 turns to the crucial applied dimension of the study by analyzing the lesson plans designed by the preservice teachers. This chapter investigates the *fidelity* of implementation — specifically, how effectively these lessons translate the Pedagogical Framework into practice and support students' K–12 AI literacy competencies. These instructional design elements are compared across the two national samples, providing a critical assessment of the program's impact on teachers' ability to transition knowledge into actionable lesson plans.

Finally, Chap. 9 provides a comprehensive synthesis and discussion of the findings from the preceding chapters. With a particular emphasis on the insights gained from comparing results across two distinct national contexts — China and the United States — this chapter critically analyzes the cultural, educational, and systemic factors that explain the observed findings. By reflecting on the application of our pedagogical framework across diverse systems, this concluding chapter contributes both empirical evidence and practical, context-specific guidance for advancing AI literacy in global teacher education.

Chapter 5
AI Literacy for Educators: Course Design and Study Participants

Abstract This chapter details the design, structure, and participant demographics of the AI Literacy for Educators course, a specialized intervention developed to prepare preservice teachers for integrating Artificial Intelligence into K–12 classrooms. The course curriculum is anchored in the Five Big Ideas in AI (Perception, Reasoning, Learning, Natural Interaction, and Societal Impact) and uses the book's Pedagogical Framework for AI Literacy to guide interdisciplinary lesson design across grade levels and core subjects. The study implemented the course in the U.S. with 31 preservice teachers and in China with 26 preservice teachers. A comparative analysis of digital usage revealed similarities in basic tool use (e.g., computers, phones) but sharp contrasts in application preference; for instance, US participants highly valued productivity apps for teaching, while Chinese participants prioritized creativity and education apps for study. Participants in both countries expressed common expectations regarding the need for practical applications and ethical understanding of AI. This chapter provides the essential context for interpreting the cross-national comparisons presented in the subsequent empirical chapters.

5.1 Introduction

In a rapidly changing educational landscape, it is becoming essential to prepare preservice teachers to effectively integrate AI into their classrooms. To address this need, educators must prioritize developing their own AI literacy—a critical step that enables them to guide students in becoming AI literate themselves, rather than simply using AI tools without a foundational understanding. This chapter describes the AI Literacy for Educators course, which was designed to equip preservice teachers with the knowledge and skills needed to do so. The content of the course is based on the Five Big Ideas in AI, providing a foundational understanding of key AI concepts, while our Pedagogical Framework for AI Literacy serves as the guide for teaching these concepts in K-12 contexts. This approach ensures that future teachers can not only become AI literate themselves but also meaningfully integrate AI literacy into their teaching.

I. Lyublinskaya and X. Du, *A Pedagogical Framework for K–12 AI Literacy*, Springer Texts in Education, https://doi.org/10.1007/978-3-032-23570-1_5

5.2 Course Objectives and Structure

The course was designed to offer educators a comprehensive exploration of AI and its transformative potential within K-12 education. It had two main objectives: to develop educators' own AI literacy and to equip them with the pedagogical knowledge and skills necessary for integrating AI literacy into their classrooms.

The course content was developed based on the Five Big Ideas in AI: Perception, Representation & Reasoning, Learning, Natural Interaction, and Societal Impact (Touretzky et al., 2023). It was structured into five distinct modules, each dedicated to a single Big Idea. These five big ideas served as the backbone of instruction, reflection, and lesson planning, ensuring coherence across sites and modules. Within each module, participants first explore core concepts through a three-step process: an introduction to the Big Idea, inquiry-based explorations using AI tools, and an analysis of the underlying principles. Throughout this process, participants are challenged to analyze the ethical implications of AI and critically evaluate its potential and challenges in education.

The focus then shifts from foundational understanding to pedagogical application. Participants gain a deep understanding of our pedagogical framework for AI literacy, which serves as the basis for integrating AI literacy into teaching and learning. They learn how to apply this framework by analyzing the connections between AI concepts and core disciplinary practices. By examining sample lessons that integrate AI literacy into standards-based curricula for different grade bands, i.e., lower elementary, upper elementary, middle, and high school, participants learn to teach AI not as an isolated topic but as an integral part of learning across disciplines. Each module culminates in an assessment task in which participants develop their own instructional units that integrate core concepts of AI's big ideas for a target audience. The finalized structure of the course is shown in Table 5.1.

Table 5.1 AI Literacy for Educators course overview

Module	Topic/Big Idea in AI	AI literacy focus	Pedagogical focus
1	Artificial Intelligence: Foundations and Societal Impact	What is AI? Societal Impact of AI	Pedagogical framework for AI literacy. AI in education
2	Perception	Sensing and Processing	AI perception: Applications to education
3	Representation and Reasoning	What is Data? Reasoning algorithms and data transformation	AI representation and reasoning: Applications to education
4	Learning	Types of machine learning. Neural networks	AI machine learning: Applications to education
5	Natural Interaction	Human–Computer Interaction. GenAI	AI natural interaction: Applications to education

Each course module was planned for 4 to 5 h of in-class instruction. Ethical reasoning was embedded across all modules, reflecting scholarly calls for AI literacy initiatives that cultivate not only technical fluency but also critical and ethical awareness. To provide a more detailed look at the course's structure, consider an example of instructional design of module 4. Specific learning objectives of this modules were:

- Explore AI core concepts, such as nature of learning, neural networks, and datasets
- Analyze different algorithms that support machine learning
- Delve deeper into workings of neural networks
- Analyze examples of K-12 lessons that integrate core concepts of machine learning
- Apply the Pedagogical Framework for AI Literacy for design of lessons that integrate the core concepts of machine learning into different disciplines

The module begins by defining core machine learning concepts and examining various types of machine learning algorithms. In small groups, participants engage in hands-on exploration of supervised, unsupervised, and reinforcement learning using online tools. For example, to explore classification as one of supervised learning algorithms, participants use Teachable Machine by Google (https://teachablemachine.withgoogle.com/) to train and test AI to recognize an image, audio, or a pose. Following this exploration, the discussion focuses on how the algorithm/model in the activity learned from the data, what types of problems or tasks a particular type of machine learning is well-suited for, what might be some of its limitations or challenges, and how it might impact people's lives or the world around us. From there, the instruction delves deeper into the inner workings of neural network architectures using online simulation tools, such as neural network playground (https://playground.tensorflow.org/). A key part of these explorations is understanding the central role that data plays in machine learning.

Following the foundational content, the module shifts its focus to pedagogical applications. Participants first discuss possible connections between the core concepts of AI learning and standards-based practices in various school disciplines. This involves reviewing diverse examples of how to integrate the core concepts of learning across different disciplines and grade bands. A key part of this section is an analysis of sample lessons that demonstrates the effective use of our Pedagogical Framework for AI Literacy. (Table 5.2).

The in-class component concludes with a small discipline-based group brainstorming session where participants discuss their individual approaches to integrating AI into a lesson of their choice. As an out-of-class module assessment, participants then apply this knowledge to develop a complete lesson plan using the Planning for AI Literacy Integration template described in Chapter 4.

Taken together, the course pedagogical approach combined conceptual grounding, hands-on practice, collaborative design, and ethical reflection. This integrated approach ensured that preservice teachers were not only introduced to AI as a technical domain but were also prepared to critically and creatively integrate AI literacy into their future teaching practice.

Table 5.2 Examples of connections between AI learning concepts and K-12 disciplinary practices

Discipline	Disciplinary practice	AI connections	Lesson example (grade band)
Mathematics	Make sense of problems and persevere in solving them	● Both AI learning and mathematical practice involve a cycle of analyzing information and trying a solution, then refining the approach based on the outcome ● Just as students analyze data and look for patterns, a machine learning model processes data to identify trends and make predictions	Lines of best fit (High school)
Science	Developing and using models	● Scientists and engineers use and construct various models based on data to represent ideas and explanations about studied phenomena ● Representing quantitative variables as data is the basis for machine learning datasets	Atomic structure of matter (Middle school)
Language arts	Clarify unknown words using context, word parts, and references, as appropriate	● Both AI learning and language arts practice refine skills by analyzing diverse data/texts ● ELA's grammar/vocabulary mirrors AI's semantic analysis for language ● Both aim for improved communication through continuous adaptation	Identifying Words with Multiple Meanings (Elementary school)
Social studies	Developing questions and planning Inquiries	● Both students and AI models engage in an iterative process of learning ● Students refine questions as they encounter new evidence ● AI models adjust their parameters to improve performance with new data	Celebrating together: Exploring cultural holidays in the U.S. (Elementary school)

5.3 Study Context and Participants

The AI Literacy for Educators course was implemented online in both the United States and China, though with differences in structure to accommodate each educational context. In each country, the course was embedded within university-based teacher education programs, though the collaborating K-12 schools were situated in diverse contexts: urban in the U.S., and a mix of urban, suburban, and rural in China. In the U.S., the course was offered for graduate credit only and was taught daily for 10 days during the winter 2025 semester, with each session lasting 2.5 h. In China, it was cross-listed as an undergraduate/graduate course and was held over a seven-week period during the summer 2025 semester, with two-hour sessions twice per week. In both cases, the course was co-taught by the two researchers.

A total of 57 educators participated in the study, with 26 participants from China and 31 participants from the United States. The side-by-side comparison of the two groups' demographics characteristics is presented in Table 5.3.

The demographic comparison highlights that the U.S. participant group ($N = 31$) was more ethnically diverse, with a composition of 29% White, 10% Black, 10% Hispanic/Latino, 45% Asian, and 6% Middle Eastern. In contrast, all Chinese participants (N = 26) were Asian (100%). Another significant difference was observed in educational backgrounds and experiences. U.S. participants were primarily graduate students (45% master's, 39% doctoral), while the majority of Chinese participants were undergraduates (62%). The U.S. group had a significantly higher percentage of degrees in STEM education (55%) compared to Chinese participants (4%). In contrast, a larger percentage of Chinese participants had degrees in Humanities and

Table 5.3 Demographics characteristics of the study participants

Demographics category	U.S. participants ($N = 31$)	Chinese participants ($N = 26$)
Ethnicity	29%	0%
● White	10%	0%
● Black	10%	0%
● Hispanic/Latino	45%	100%
● Asian	6%	0%
● Middle Eastern		
Degree program enrollment	0%	62%
● Undergraduate	45%	38%
● Masters	39%	0%
● Doctoral	16%	0%
● None		
Education-specific degree	55%	4%
● STEM education	6%	19%
● Humanities & arts education	3%	0%
● Special education	10%	31%
● Educational foundations	6%	4%
Non-educational degrees	10%	19%
● STEM	10%	12%
● Humanities and arts	0%	4%
● Social sciences	0%	7%
● Professional/vocational		
● Undeclared		
Prior teaching experience	16%	65%
● None	42%	27%
● K-12	42%	8%
● College level		
Industry work experience	48%	62%
● None	3%	31%
● Less than 2 years	19%	7%
● 2 - 5 years	30%	0%
● Over 5 years		
First generation college students	35%	31%

arts education (19%) and Educational foundations (31%), compared to U.S. participants (6% and 10% respectively). In terms of prior experience, a higher percentage of U.S. participants had K-12 (42%) and college-level (42%) teaching experience, while the majority of Chinese participants had no prior teaching experience (65%). Similarly, 62% of Chinese participants had no industry work experience, compared to 48% of their U.S. counterparts. A notable similarity between the two groups was the percentage of first-generation college students, with 35% of U.S. participants and 31% of Chinese participants identifying as such.

The following section provides a comparative analysis of the U.S. and Chinese participants' digital experiences prior to the enrollment in the course.

5.4 A Comparative Analysis of Digital Technology Use and Course Expectations of the U.S. and Chinese Participants

Participants' prior experience with digital technology and their expectations for the course were gathered using the survey. The first section of the survey included multiple-select questions to document their familiarity with a variety of digital tools and applications, asking them to indicate specific contexts in which they use them, for example, teaching, studying, or entertainment. The second section included an open-ended question to capture participants' learning goals and desired outcomes for the course.

5.4.1 Use of Digital Tools

The side-by-side comparison of the percentages of the U.S. and Chinese participants reporting using various digital tools in different contexts is shown in Table 5.4.

In order to identify major differences and similarities in the data reported by the U.S. and Chinese participants (Table 5.4), we implemented the following classification. If fewer than 25% of participants reported using a particular digital tool in a specific context, we categorized that as minimal. From 25 to 49% of participants we considered it to be low. From 50 to 74% we considered it to be moderate. Finally, if 75% or more participants used a particular digital tool in a specific context, we categorized that as high.

A comparative analysis of digital tool usage between U.S. and Chinese participants reveals both notable similarities and significant differences based on the number of participants who reported using them. In both groups, a high number of participants reported using computers and phones for daily tasks, such as studying at home (US: 100% and CN: 92% for computer use; US: 77% and CN: 92% for phone use) and entertainment (US: 84% and CN: 92% for phone use). In both cohorts, a high number

Table 5.4 Comparison of prior use of digital tools for U.S. ($N = 31$) and Chinese ($N = 26$) participants

Digital tools	Contexts of using digital tools						
	Study in school	Study at home	Entertainment	Leisure reading	Health/ physical activity	Other	Not using/ do not own
Computer	US: 84% CN: 96%	US:100% CN: 92%	US: 81% CN: 77%	US: 65% CN: 62%	US: 39% CN: 27%	US: 6% CN: 8%	US: 0% CN: 0%
Phone	US: 68% CN: 81%	US: 77% CN: 92%	US: 84% CN: 92%	US: 65% CN: 77%	US: 65% CN: 65%	US: 16% CN: 31%	US: 0% CN: 0%
Smart home device	US: NA CN: NA	US: 35% CN: 58%	US: 45% CN: 35%	US: 13% CN: 23%	US: 6% CN: 19%	US: 39% CN: 15%	US: 6% CN: 12%
Tablet	US: 58% CN: 85%	US: 71% CN: 92%	US: 45% CN: 81%	US: 52% CN: 46%	US: 23% CN: 23%	US: 26% CN: 12%	US: 10% CN: 4%
TV	US: 16% CN: 31%	US: 29% CN: 54%	US: 87% CN: 85%	US: 6% CN: 12%	US: 16% CN: 15%	US: 13% CN: 12%	US: 3% CN: 4%
Gaming console	US: 3% CN: 6%	US: 6% CN: 19%	US: 52% CN: 69%	US: 3% CN: 8%	US: 6% CN: 15%	US: 29% CN: 19%	US: 16% CN: 15%
Wearables	US: 10% CN: 31%	US: 13% CN: 31%	US: 13% CN: 33%	US: 6% CN: 12%	US: 48% CN: 58%	US: 26% CN: 12%	US: 19% CN: 19%
Other	US: 10% CN: 31%	US: 26% CN: 27%	US: 10% CN: 19%	US: 3% CN: 15%	US: 0% CN: 15%	US: 52% CN: 35%	US: 29% CN: 35%

of participants also reported using TVs for entertainment (US: 87% and CN: 85%). Additionally, in both groups a minimal number of participants reported using gaming consoles for studying at school (US: 3% and CN: 6%) and for leisure reading (US: 3% and CN: 8%). The data also highlights distinct differences between the two groups. A particularly sharp contrast is seen in the use of tablets for entertainment. A high number of Chinese participants reported using them (81%), while only a moderate number of U.S. participants did so (45%). Another significant difference lies in the use of gaming consoles and wearables for health and fitness. A minimal to low number of U.S. participants reported using these tools for this purpose (6% for gaming consoles, 48% for wearables), whereas a low to moderate number of Chinese participants reported their use (15% for gaming consoles, 58% for wearables).

5.4.2 Use of Digital Applications

We will now provide a more detailed look at the specific digital applications both the U.S. and Chinese participants reported using (Table 5.5), offering deeper insights into their day-to-day digital preferences.

A comparative analysis of digital applications usage between U.S. and Chinese participants indicated the following similarities and significant differences based on the number of participants who reported using them. In both groups, a high number of participants reported using for personal use social media and communication apps (US: 87%, CN: 100%), entertainment apps (US: 100%, CN: 96%), productivity and business apps (US: 100%, CN: 96%), and utility and tools apps (US: 77%, CN: 77%). Other notable similarities included a low number of participants in both groups who reported using social media and communication applications in contexts other than personal use, study, or teaching (US: 6%, CN: 8%), and the fact that 100% of participants in both cohorts use productivity and business, and entertainment apps for some purpose.

The data also highlights distinct differences between the two groups. For studying, a high number of Chinese participants reported using entertainment apps (96%),

Table 5.5 Comparison of prior use of digital applications for U.S. ($N = 31$) and Chinese ($N = 26$) participants

Digital applications	Context of using digital applications				
	Personal	Study	Teaching	Other	Do not use
Social & communication	US: 87% CN: 100%	US: 23% CN: 58%	US: 19% CN: 27%	US: 6% CN: 8%	US: 13% CN: 0%
Entertainment	US: 100% CN: 96%	US: 26% CN: 96%	US: 29% CN: 50%	US: 10% CN: 19%	US: 0% CN: 0%
Education	US: 55% CN: 54%	US: 65% CN: 88%	US: 39% CN: 23%	US: 6% CN: 4%	US: 19% CN: 0%
Productivity & business	US: 100% CN: 96%	US: 77% CN: 46%	US: 74% CN: 23%	US: 13% CN: 15%	US: 0% CN: 0%
Utility & Tools	US: 77% CN: 77%	US: 26% CN: 35%	US: 10% CN: 23%	US: 3% CN: 12%	US: 23% CN: 3%
Creativity	US: 45% CN: 73%	US: 32% CN: 77%	US: 35% CN: 31%	US: 6% CN: 12%	US: 39% CN: 12%
Other	US: 29% CN: 42%	US: 16% CN: 23%	US: 13% CN: 19%	US: 10% CN: 23%	US: 55% CN: 38%

whereas a minimal number of U.S. participants did so (26%). Similarly, for studying, a high number of Chinese participants used education apps (88%), while a moderate number of U.S. participants did so (65%). Another significant difference is seen in the use of productivity and business apps for teaching, with a high number of U.S. participants (74%) reporting this use, compared to a minimal number of Chinese participants (23%). A high number of Chinese participants use creativity apps for studying (77%) and for personal use (73%) compared to the US participants (32% and 45%, respectively). On the other hand, a high number of US participants use productivity and business apps for studying (77%) and for teaching (74%) compared to Chinese participants (46% and 23%, respectively).

These findings indicate different patterns in how each group integrates specific digital tools and applications into their lives and provide important context for the cross-national findings presented in Chapters 6 - 8 of the book.

5.4.3 Course Expectations

To gain a deeper understanding of the course expectations of each cohort, a thematic analysis was conducted on the open-ended survey responses from both U.S. and Chinese participants. This analysis identified and compared the emergent themes, revealing both shared priorities and distinct perspectives on the role of artificial intelligence in education. The two common themes that emerged from the responses were *practical applications of AI in education* and *Ethical and societal implications of AI technology.*

Many participants expressed a desire to learn how to apply AI in a school or classroom setting, both for themselves and for their students: "I want to learn more about AI to enhance my learning process, as well as combine AI with my research interests in climate change education and education for sustainable development". (U.S. participant) Some participants expressed a more general interest in learning about the role of AI in education:

> I want to learn about Artificial Intelligence in general, of its potentials and limitations. As our world and technology is evolving, I want to be able to integrate the benefits of AI in my classroom and perhaps in my daily life as well. (U.S. participant)

Others indicated their interest to learn about specific examples of AI applications in the classroom focusing on how to integrate them into teaching and how they can simplify or improve the learning process as evident from the following statements: "As a teacher curious about AI, I'm excited to see how it can spice up my classroom with personalized learning and cool tech tools." (U.S. participant). This also included expectations to learn about integrating AI into teaching practices and using it to improve learning outcomes: "I'm specifically interested in what types of AI technology can be used in teaching and learning." (Chinese participant).

> I want to know the difference between traditional teaching and teaching with the help of [AI] technology, and I think the application of technology in teaching is also very important, which accelerates students' understanding. (Chinese participant)

The concern for the ethical use of AI and its impact on society, the nature of knowledge, and human culture was another recurring theme for both the U.S. and Chinese participants. Many statements indicated participants' interest in understanding the potential risks and liabilities of AI: "I am fascinated by the profound questions AI raises about the essence of humanity, the meaning of existence and knowledge, the transformation of future life forms, and the potential evolution of human cultural heritage." (U.S. participant) Many participants also showed an awareness of the broader implications of AI, including its potential to change the fundamental nature of education: "It can be used in ethical ways to benefit students and teachers, but if used unethically or if completely avoided, it seems to have a pervasive nature in the way that students use it to cut corners and avoid deeper learning." (U.S. participant), "I'm interested in how AI can support education without causing new problems, like making learning more fair and accessible, but also avoiding bias or replacing real human connection." (Chinese participant).

Each cohort also had themes that were distinctive for them. Two teacher-related themes emerged from the responses of the U.S. participants: *enhancing productivity and systematic use of AI technology* and *automating administrative tasks*. Several U.S. participants indicated their desire to move beyond a casual understanding of AI and learn how to use it more methodically and systematically for professional and personal productivity, including tasks like curriculum and content development: "I want to know how AI can help me strategically learn, generate information, accelerate decision-making skills, and develop curriculum better, including designing activities, choosing or generating better learning materials, designing assessment tools, and creating written documents." (U.S. participant). U.S. participants also highlighted a very specific and practical use case for AI in a professional setting to make administrative tasks more efficient.

> As a childcare center owner, I hope this class can give me some ideas about how to integrate AI into my center. I want to use AI to help automate administrative tasks, such as attendance tracking, fee management, and even communication with parents. (U.S. participant)

The distinctive theme that emerged from Chinese participants' responses represented their desire to acquire *fundamental knowledge about AI* and about the role of AI in *enhancing engagement and learning outcomes of the students*. The first theme represented participants' need to become AI literate in order to build a solid base for future learning and development: "I haven't learned any related AI knowledge before and I want to have a deeper understanding and grasp the basic knowledge." (Chinese participant). The second theme indicated Chinese participants' interest to learn about how AI can be used to make education more engaging and effective, with a specific focus on student learning outcomes and classroom dynamics: "It would be great to go beyond the theoretical aspects of learning technology and dive deep into the application of learning technology in real world experience and student learning outcomes." (Chinese participant).

In summary, a comparative analysis of the two cohorts' characteristics reveals both shared patterns and important contrasts. While their fundamental use of digital tools and applications for everyday tasks is very similar, their specific preferences and areas of focus differ significantly. These distinctions, along with the varying course expectations highlighted by both cohorts, provide an essential baseline for interpreting the subsequent findings related to AI competence and ethical awareness development and instructional design, offering crucial context for the cross-national comparisons presented in the following chapters of the book.

Reference

Touretzky, D., Gardner-McCune, C., & Seehorn, D. (2023). Machine learning and the five big ideas in AI. *International Journal of Artificial Intelligence in Education, 33*(2), 233–266. https://doi.org/10.1007/s40593-022-00314-1

Chapter 6
Examining Chinese and American Preservice Teachers' AI Content Knowledge

Abstract This chapter presents an empirical study examining the direct impact of the AI Literacy for Educators course on preservice teachers' foundational AI content knowledge. Using a non-equivalent group pre/post quasi-experimental design (N = 53), the study assessed changes in knowledge related to the Five Big Ideas in AI (Perception, Representation & Reasoning, Learning, Natural Interaction, and Societal Impact) across cohorts from the United States and China. The instrument was developed with strong content validity, aligning directly with the Five Big Ideas in AI framework. Results indicated that both the U.S. and Chinese cohorts achieved statistically significant, medium-sized gains in overall AI content knowledge. A Multivariate Analysis of Covariance (MANCOVA) revealed no significant difference in final adjusted post-test scores between the cohorts after controlling for baseline knowledge, confirming the content transferability of the Five Big Ideas in AI framework across diverse educational contexts. Descriptive analysis, however, showed divergent patterns of conceptual growth: the U.S. cohort excelled in Representation & Reasoning, while the Chinese cohort demonstrated the largest growth in Learning and Perception, reflecting the course's effectiveness in closing specific, pre-existing knowledge gaps. This study affirms that utilizing the Five Big Ideas in AI as a content anchor in a systematic curriculum is effective in building the robust, interdisciplinary content foundation necessary for teachers' AI literacy.

6.1 Introduction

In Chap. 5, we established the foundation for our comparative studies by detailing the design and implementation of the AI Literacy for Educators course, which served as our pedagogical intervention. This course was created to equip preservice teachers from the United States and China with the essential knowledge and skills needed to effectively integrate AI literacy into K-12 education. As we established in Chap. 2, a comprehensive model of AI literacy is multidimensional, requiring not just the ability to critically use and ethically evaluate AI, but also basic technical understanding of AI. This foundational knowledge serves as the content anchor of our

I. Lyublinskaya and X. Du, *A Pedagogical Framework for K–12 AI Literacy*, Springer Texts in Education, https://doi.org/10.1007/978-3-032-23570-1_6

multidimensional model of AI literacy, ensuring that future educators possess the necessary understanding of how AI works to integrate these concepts across the K-12 curriculum effectively and responsibly. Without this core competence, attempts at critical evaluation and instructional design risk becoming superficial or reliant on misinformation, highlighting the necessity of assessing this content anchor as the first step in our empirical inquiry.

Thus, in this chapter, we transition to an empirical investigation of the direct impact of this course on one of the critical components of AI literacy: content knowledge. This knowledge is not merely academic; it is the essential prerequisite that enables educators to move beyond simple tool use and instead guide students toward becoming AI-literate citizens. Therefore, assessing the development of content knowledge related to the Five Big Ideas in AI (Perception, Representation & Reasoning, Learning, Natural Interaction, and Societal Impact) is the central focus of this chapter. By measuring the change in participants' understanding of AI's core concepts, we investigate the course's effectiveness and how contextual factors may influence the development of these competencies in two distinct national cohorts.

6.2 Methodology

This study follows a non-equivalent group pre/post quasi-experimental design and is guided by the following research questions:

1. To what extent did preservice teachers in China and the United States improve their AI content knowledge following participation in the course?
2. How did learning gains vary across the Five Big Ideas in AI?
3. Were there significant differences in the comparative learning gains between the two national contexts?

6.2.1 Participants

The participants for this study were drawn from the two international cohorts of preservice teachers who enrolled in the AI Literacy for Educators course, with initial demographics detailed in Chap. 5. As a reminder, the U.S. cohort was notably more ethnically diverse, and participants were primarily graduate students (45% master's, 39% doctoral) with higher rates of prior K-12 (42%) and college-level (42%) teaching experience. In contrast, the Chinese cohort largely consisted of undergraduates (62%), all of whom were Asian (100%), and the majority reported no prior teaching experience (65%).

The full study population for the course comprised 57 preservice teachers ($N = 31$ U.S., $N = 26$ Chinese). However, as is common in educational research involving pre- and post-testing, a subset of participants did not complete both the initial pre-test and the final post-test instruments necessary for calculating reliable knowledge gains. Therefore, for the quantitative analysis presented in this chapter, we excluded participants with incomplete data sets to maintain statistical integrity. This resulted in a final analytical sample of 52 participants (N = 28 U.S. participants and N = 24 Chinese participants). All subsequent results and findings are based on this refined sample size, ensuring a direct and valid comparison of content knowledge acquisition between the two cohorts.

6.2.2 *Research Instrument*

The content knowledge of participants was assessed using a multiple-choice test developed specifically for this study. This instrument was designed as the content anchor for our multidimensional model of AI literacy, ensuring future educators possessed the foundational understanding necessary for effective and responsible integration across the K-12 curriculum. The test consisted of 20 multiple-choice questions, each providing five response options, including the "I don't know" option to distinguish between incorrect knowledge and a lack of knowledge. This design ensured a more accurate measure of genuine learning gains. The test was directly aligned with the Five Big Ideas in AI (Perception, Representation & Reasoning, Learning, Natural Interaction, and Societal Impact) which also served as the structural backbone for the five instructional modules of the course (Touretzky et al., 2023). The test was divided into five sections, with four questions dedicated to each of the Big Ideas, collectively measuring participants' understanding of the core concepts described by the framework.

The Perception subscale (Items 1–4) assessed participants' understanding of how AI systems sense, capture, and interpret data from the physical world through modalities such as vision, sound, and touch. Items targeted core perceptual processes, including computer vision, speech recognition, data encoding, and sensor integration, as well as practical challenges such as noise, occlusion, and lighting variation that affect performance in real-world environments. This subscale emphasized the foundational link between sensing mechanisms and downstream reasoning, establishing how AI "senses" and "perceives" the world as a precursor to understanding and decision-making.

The Representation & Reasoning subscale (Items 5–8) focused on how AI systems encode knowledge and perform logical inference to solve problems. Items addressed symbolic AI, logic programming, semantic networks, and inductive versus deductive reasoning, asking participants to match reasoning strategies to different problem types or to select appropriate data structures for specific decision-making contexts. This subscale directly assessed participants' understanding of the relationship between how knowledge is structured and how conclusions are drawn, emphasizing reasoning as a bridge between data and action.

The Learning subscale (Items 9–12) measured participants' comprehension of machine learning principles and processes, including supervised, unsupervised, and reinforcement learning, as well as neural networks and the role of data in model development. Items assessed understanding of overfitting, generalization, and the trade-offs between model accuracy, interpretability, and computational cost. This subscale captured participants' understanding of how AI systems improve performance through experience, a critical conceptual shift for preservice teachers to understand the adaptive nature of AI and its pedagogical analogues in human learning.

The Natural Interaction subscale (Items 13–16) evaluated knowledge of how AI systems communicate and collaborate with humans through natural language processing, voice and gesture recognition, and multimodal interfaces. Items examined interface design, accessibility, and the ethical dimensions of usability, prompting participants to differentiate between systems that process single versus multiple input modalities and to identify design features that promote equitable interaction. This subscale emphasized the interplay between technical design and human experience, an essential bridge between computational systems and educational contexts.

The Societal Impact subscale (Items 17–20) examined participants' awareness of ethical, cultural, and civic dimensions of AI use. Items explored issues of fairness, transparency, privacy, accountability, and bias in algorithmic systems, as well as broader implications such as job displacement, surveillance, and digital inequality. Participants analyzed the potential benefits and risks of AI for education and society, identifying ethical concerns, such as how automated assessment tools might inadvertently reinforce social inequities, and proposing ways to mitigate them. This subscale assessed preservice teachers' understanding of potential implications of AI technologies in schools and communities.

Finally, while the analytic sample size was too small to conduct robust statistical validation procedures, such as Exploratory or Confirmatory Factor Analysis (EFA/CFA), and a formal expert evaluation was not feasible, the test's rigor rests on its strong content validity. The instrument's development was meticulously aligned with the Five Big Ideas in AI framework (Touretzky et al., 2023), which is the widely accepted national guideline for K-12 AI education. Because the course curriculum itself was structured entirely around these same five ideas, the test items possess inherent content relevance and representativeness. We argue that this close, pre-established alignment with a consensus-driven framework is sufficient to establish content validity for measuring the knowledge gains specifically targeted by this pedagogical intervention. The specific conceptual focus and item distribution for each of the Five Big Ideas, along with representative sample questions, are summarized in Table 6.1.

6.2.3 Procedure

The AI content knowledge test was administered to all participants at two time points to measure knowledge change across the intervention period. The test was administered as a pre-test prior to the first session of the course for each cohort to establish baseline content knowledge. The post-test was administered after the final session of the course to capture knowledge improvement. Both assessments were

Table 6.1 Alignment of AI Content Knowledge Test with AI's Big Ideas

Big Idea in AI	Sample test questions	Focus
Perception	Q3. In the context of AI and perception, what is the term used for the process of converting raw sensory data into a format a computer can understand and use?	Techniques for perception tasks, challenges in real-world environments, sensory data conversion, and applications of computer vision
Representation and Reasoning	Q5. Which of the following is NOT a common approach used for representing knowledge in AI systems?	Approaches for knowledge representation, definitions of symbolic AI
	Q7. Which of the following is an example of reasoning in an AI system?	Examples of reasoning in an AI system and common reasoning techniques
Learning	Q9. In supervised learning, the AI system is provided with:	Components of supervised learning (e.g., Question 9),
	Q11. Overfitting in machine learning occurs when:	Types of machine learning algorithms, concepts of model generalization such as overfitting and the role of data
Natural Interaction	Q16. Which of the following is an example of a multimodal AI system?	Key considerations in Natural Language Processing (NLP), challenges in speech recognition systems, aspects of user-friendly AI interface design, and examples of multimodal AI systems
Societal Impact	Q18. Which of the following is NOT an ethical consideration related to AI development?	Potential societal benefits and ethical considerations
	Q19. How can bias in training data lead to biased outcomes in AI systems?	The mechanism of bias in training data and challenges in ensuring fairness and transparency

completed by participants online under similar time constraints. The administration procedure was consistent across cohorts, but the intervening pedagogical treatment period differed due to the non-equivalent course structures.

For the U.S. cohort, the course was implemented in an intensive, condensed format, taught daily over 10 days during the Winter 2025 semester, with each session lasting 2.5 h. The pre- and post-tests thus bracketed a two-week period. For the Chinese cohort, the course followed a spaced format, held over a seven-week period during the Summer 2025 semester, with two-hour sessions delivered twice per week. The pre- and post-tests thus bracketed a seven-week period. Despite these differences in pacing and duration, which are acknowledged as contextual factors that may influence comparative learning gains, the core content based on the Five Big Ideas in AI and the co-teaching personnel remained consistent across both implementations.

All datasets were de-identified prior to analysis, and country-level codes were used solely to distinguish cohorts for comparative purposes. Responses were stored securely on password-protected institutional servers, with demographic information maintained in a separate file to ensure participant confidentiality and data integrity.

6.2.4 *Data Analysis*

Data analysis was conducted in a multi-stage process using SPSS 30 to address the three primary research questions regarding learning gains and cross-national differences.

To address RQ1: *To what extent did preservice teachers in China and the United States improve their AI content knowledge following participation in the course?* means, standard deviations, and score ranges were calculated for the overall total score on both the pre-test and post-test, separately for the U.S. and Chinese cohorts. To determine the statistical significance of the change, a paired-samples t-test was performed on the overall total test score for each cohort. Effect sizes were calculated using Cohen's d for repeated measures to assess the magnitude of the observed learning gains.

To address RQ2: *How did learning gains vary across the Five Big Ideas in AI?* descriptive statistics were calculated for each of the five subscales on the pre-test and post-test for each cohort. The analysis of subscale gain scores was used to create radar plots, visually depicting the comparative domain-level conceptual growth patterns between the two cohorts. Subscale-level inferential tests were addressed in the multivariate approach for RQ3.

To address RQ3: *Were there significant differences in the comparative learning gains between the two national contexts?* a multivariate analysis of covariance (MANCOVA) was employed with the five post-test domain scores as the dependent variables, the corresponding five pre-test scores as covariates in the model, and the country as the independent variable.

6.3 Results

The findings of the empirical study are reported following the order of the research questions outlined in the Methodology. We begin by presenting descriptive statistics on the overall pre- and post-test scores for each cohort and then detail the statistically significant within-group improvements demonstrated by both cohorts (RQ1). We then explore the differential learning gains across the Five Big Ideas in AI using descriptive and visual methods (RQ2). Finally, we present the results of the multivariate analysis of covariance (MANCOVA) to determine if there were significant differences in comparative learning gains between the two national contexts (RQ3).

6.3.1 Overall Improvement in AI Content Knowledge (RQ1)

To address the first research question, descriptive statistics for the total pre- and post-test scores and the paired-samples t-tests were conducted for each cohort. The results of calculations are presented for both cohorts in Table 6.2.

Descriptive statistics for the total test score (out of 20) revealed that both cohorts began the course with a similar baseline level of knowledge. The Chinese cohort (N = 24) scored an average of M = 14.79 (SD = 4.25) on the pre-test, while the U.S. cohort (N = 29) scored marginally higher at M = 14.90 (SD = 3.88). A strong positive correlation was found between the pre- and post-test scores for both groups (.727 and .621 for Chinese and American cohorts, respectively), confirming the stability of relative knowledge rankings over the course period. Following the intervention, both groups demonstrated statistically significant learning gains. The Chinese participants' mean score increased to M = 16.50 (SD = 5.24), resulting in a statistically significant improvement, $t(23) = -2.306$, $p = .015$, with a medium effect size, Cohen's $d = 0.47$. Similarly, the U.S. participants' mean score increased to M = 17.14 (SD = 4.726), also indicating a statistically significant improvement, $t(28) = -3.158$, $p = .002$ with a moderate effect size, Cohen's $d = 0.59$. In summary, both the Chinese and U.S. preservice teachers experienced a statistically significant, medium-sized increase in their overall AI content knowledge after completing the AI Literacy for Educators course.

Table 6.2 Descriptive statistics and paired samples *t*-test results for Chinese and US cohorts

		Pre-test		Post-test					
Country	N	M	SD	M	SD	*t*	df	Sig. (two-tailed)	Cohen's *d*
China	24	14.79	4.253	16.50	5.242	-2.306	23	.030	.47
U.S	29	14.90	3.876	17.14	4.726	-3.157	28	.004	.59

Table 6.2 Descriptive Statistics for Five Big Ideas Subscales

	China				U.S			
	Pre-test		Post-test		Pre-test		Post-test	
Big Idea in AI	M	SD	M	SD	M	SD	M	SD
Perception	2.71	1.12	3.25	.99	2.69	.81	3.28	1.13
Representation and Reasoning	3.00	1.02	3.17	1.31	2.59	1.27	3.34	1.23
Learning	2.67	1.37	3.21	1.35	3.10	.94	3.34	1.01
Natural Interaction	3.04	1.20	3.42	1.06	3.24	.91	3.59	.95
Societal Impact	3.37	.88	3.46	1.02	3.28	1.03	3.59	1.05

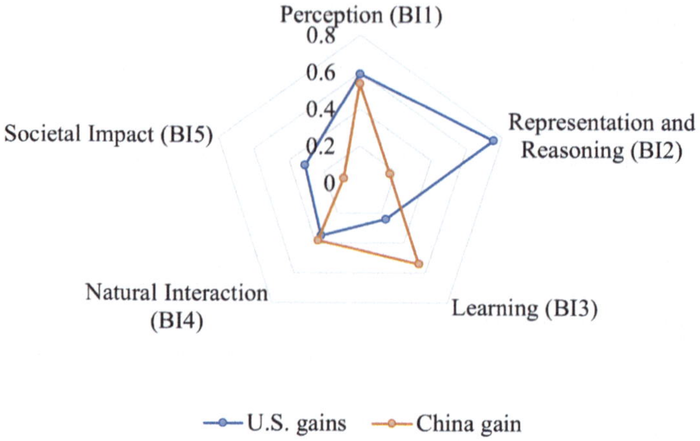

Fig. 6.1 Comparative gains across the Five Big Ideas in AI

6.3.2 *Domain-Specific Patterns of Knowledge Growth (RQ2)*

To examine how learning gains varied across the Five Big Ideas in AI, pre- and post-test descriptive statistics were calculated for each of the five subscales to reveal domain-specific shifts in content knowledge (Table 6.2).

Analysis of the domain-specific scores revealed distinct patterns of conceptual growth. Consistent with the overall positive effect, all five subscales showed an increase in mean scores for both the U.S. and Chinese cohorts. However, the magnitude of these gains varied considerably across the domains. For the Chinese cohort, the most substantial learning gains were observed in the Perception (BI1) and Learning (BI3), while the smallest gain was recorded in the Societal Impact (BI5). Conversely, the U.S. cohort demonstrated its largest growth in the Representation and Reasoning (BI2), while the smallest gains were observed in the Learning (BI3).

To visually compare these domain-level conceptual changes, the gain scores for both cohorts were plotted onto a radar chart (Fig. 6.1). This visualization clearly depicts the non-uniform nature of the learning process, highlighting which of the Five Big Ideas were most and least influenced by the course intervention within each national context.

6.3.3 *Comparative Analysis of Learning Gains Between National Cohorts (RQ3)*

To compare the learning gains between the two national contexts, a MANCOVA was employed using SPSS 30. This model included the five post-test subscale scores as dependent variables, country (U.S. vs. China) as the independent variable, and the five corresponding pre-test subscale scores as covariates to control for initial knowledge differences. The MANCOVA indicated no statistically significant multivariate effect of the country on the combined set of post-test subscale scores, $F(5, 42) = .753$, $p = .764$ (Wilks' $\lambda = .918$). This finding suggests that, after statistically controlling for pre-existing knowledge differences, the U.S. and Chinese cohorts did not differ significantly in their overall pattern of conceptual learning gains across the Five Big Ideas in AI. While the descriptive data (Table 6.2 and Fig. 6.1) suggested divergent patterns of conceptual growth (i.e., the U.S. excelled in Representation & Reasoning, while China excelled in Perception and Learning), these differences in raw gain magnitudes were not significant enough to translate into statistically different final knowledge levels when initial baseline scores were accounted for.

6.4 Discussion

The present study provides compelling empirical evidence that a course structured around the Five Big Ideas in AI can effectively enhance preservice teachers' AI content knowledge across two distinct national contexts. Both U.S. ($d = 0.59$) and Chinese ($d = 0.47$) participants demonstrated statistically significant, medium-sized gains from pre- to post-test, confirming that explicit, conceptually organized instruction leads to building a robust and transferrable understanding of AI. Consistent with prior research, these results reinforce the notion that intentional and scaffolded learning experiences, rather than incidental exposure through everyday technology use, are necessary for future educators to engage meaningfully with both the technical foundations and the societal implications of AI (Dilek et al., 2025; Sperling et al., 2024). While Chap. 5 documented that participants' familiarity with AI was uneven and often limited to consumer-level interactions, this chapter demonstrates that a systematic, conceptually organized curriculum aimed at developing teachers' AI content knowledge can effectively translate abstract AI concepts into concrete, teachable learning experiences that support long-term conceptual understanding.

6.4.1 *Contextual Factors and Learning Patterns*

The study findings indicated the absence of a statistically significant multivariate effect of the country on the adjusted post-test scores ($F(5, 42) = 0.50$, $p = .764$). This suggests that the course curriculum is pedagogically coherent, culturally adaptable, and highly transferable, achieving comparable final knowledge levels across institutional and cultural boundaries after controlling for initial baseline knowledge. This result resonates with UNESCO's global call for AI literacy that balances universal conceptual anchors with local adaptability (Miao & Cukurova, 2024). Yet, the descriptive contrasts (Table 6.2 and Fig. 6.1) between cohorts reveal how learning contexts, disciplinary preparation, and course structure shape the patterns of learning gains:

- U.S. Cohort: The U.S. cohort displayed the most significant raw gain in Representation & Reasoning (BI2) ($\Delta M = 0.75$), effectively closing the deficit in their lowest baseline domain ($M_{pre} = 2.59$ out of 4.0). Their intensive 10-day course format likely encouraged rapid conceptual synthesis, aligning with their professional maturity and strong existing analytical skills.
- Chinese Cohort: The largest raw gains ($\Delta M = 0.54$) were observed in both the Learning (BI3) and Perception (BI1) subscales. The substantial growth in Learning effectively addressed their lowest baseline score ($M_{pre} = 2.67$ out of 4.0). Conversely, the smallest gain ($\Delta M = 0.09$) was in Societal Impact (BI5). This minimal gain is attributable to a likely ceiling effect, as the Chinese cohort exhibited their highest pre-test mean score in this domain ($M_{pre} = 3.37$ out of 4.0), leaving little room for further conceptual growth.

These contrasts suggest that disciplinary background, course pacing, and digital practices interact dynamically with the structure of AI literacy instruction. The U.S. course functioned as an accelerated conceptual immersion, leveraging professional maturity and technical readiness, while the Chinese course fostered iterative reflection through discussion and contextualized examples. Both patterns were effective but differently paced—one emphasizing synthesis and application, the other emphasizing conceptual foundational building. Together, these findings affirm that AI literacy is contextually constructed: its development depends on the interplay between the learner's disciplinary lens, the instructional design, and the sociocultural norms of teaching and learning.

6.4.2 Pedagogical and Theoretical Contributions

By connecting the design features outlined in Chap. 5 to the learning outcomes examined in this study, the findings illustrate how the Five Big Ideas in AI serve as a conceptual and pedagogical bridge between theory and practice. The framework successfully anchors the content dimension of our multidimensional AI literacy model, ensuring that the necessary technical and ethical foundations are systematically covered. This rigor is key: the coherence and universality of the Five Big Ideas in AI unify instruction across its technical, ethical, and pedagogical components, providing the conceptual foundation necessary to integrate the pedagogical and critical dimensions in diverse educational settings. This dual capacity for coherence and flexibility positions the Five Big Ideas as an essential content model for AI literacy development within teacher education, one that ensures conceptual rigor without sacrificing contextual relevance.

In pedagogical terms, our Pedagogical Framework for AI Literacy embodies what this book terms scaffolded conceptual progression: a structured pathway through which learners advance from surface familiarity to structured understanding and finally to applied reasoning. This progression mirrors the cognitive trajectory advocated by recent research on conceptual learning in technology education (Ng et al., 2024), emphasizing that deep AI literacy emerges when abstract concepts are situated within meaningful, practice-based contexts. The results of this study confirm that by utilizing the Five Big Ideas in AI as the content anchor within this framework, we can effectively operationalize this progression across distinct cultural and disciplinary environments, helping preservice teachers internalize complex foundational concepts through guided inquiry and reflection.

Theoretically, the study contributes to growing scholarship on the content knowledge component of AI literacy as a multifaceted construct that integrates cognitive, ethical, and sociocultural dimensions. Rather than treating AI content knowledge as a discrete set of technical skills, the findings reinforce that a robust content base is critical for teachers to interpret, apply, and critique AI systems through both computational and humanistic lenses. The Five Big Ideas in AI framework thus provides a demonstrated conceptual architecture for content knowledge that can systematically accommodate both algorithmic understanding and ethical–societal reflection. Moreover, the Five Big Ideas framework advances a pedagogical theory of content transferability in AI literacy—showing that these core conceptual structures can remain stable and highly effective even when implemented in different national or institutional contexts, as evidenced by the statistically comparable adjusted post-test scores. The comparable post-test gains across U.S. and Chinese cohorts suggest that the Five Big Ideas function as flexible yet coherent constructs that enable collaboration across cultural and disciplinary divides.

Another key insight emerging from the study is the pedagogical value of disciplinary diversity. Our findings indicate that STEM-oriented participants demonstrated greater facility in computational reasoning and humanities-oriented participants showed high initial content knowledge in ethical interpretation, resulting in less overall gains. The complementary strengths observed across cohorts highlight that effective AI content knowledge development thrives at the intersection of disciplines. This finding aligns with contemporary theories of interdisciplinary cognition, suggesting that deep understanding arises when learners reconcile multiple epistemic perspectives. (Mansilla & Duraising, 2007; Nikitina, 2005).

6.4.3 Limitations of the Study

Several limitations warrant consideration. First, the sample size ($N = 53$) was modest and limited to two institutional contexts, which restricts generalizability. Future research should replicate this study with larger, more diverse cohorts to enable robust inferential analyses and cross-cultural comparisons. Second, the AI content knowledge test used in this study was researcher-developed and exploratory, designed to capture early indicators of AI knowledge growth. While it demonstrated strong content validity through alignment with the Five Big Ideas in AI, the small sample precluded formal construct validation (e.g., confirmatory factor analysis). Finally, while the study controlled for baseline knowledge, instructional and linguistic differences between the U.S. and Chinese versions of the course may have influenced outcomes, serving as an important contextual constraint when interpreting the comparable final post-test scores.

6.5 Conclusions

In sum, the study affirms that the Five Big Ideas in AI provide a durable, flexible, and pedagogically sound foundation for AI content knowledge in teacher education. The intervention resulted in statistically significant, medium-sized AI content knowledge gains in both the U.S. and Chinese cohorts (RQ1), with no statistically significant difference in final adjusted knowledge levels across the two national contexts (RQ3). When implemented through a coherent curriculum that combines conceptual depth, ethical awareness, and contextual sensitivity, the use of Five Big Ideas in AI as a content anchor enables preservice teachers to become not merely users of AI but informed, reflective, and adaptive educators. The findings presented in this chapter are a significant contribution to the scholarship on AI literacy, demonstrating both the content transferability of the Five Big Ideas in AI framework across distinct educational systems and the pedagogical value of interdisciplinary grounding for teachers' AI content knowledge development. As AI continues to reshape educational practice, the ability to interpret, evaluate, and guide its use becomes a defining feature of teacher professionalism.

References

Dilek, M., Baran, E., & Aleman, E. (2025). AI literacy in teacher education: Empowering educators through critical co-discovery. *Journal of Teacher Education, 76*(3), 294–311. https://doi.org/10.1177/00224871251325083

Mansilla, V. B., & Duraising, E. D. (2007). Targeted assessment of students' interdisciplinary work: An empirically grounded framework proposed. *The Journal of Higher Education, 78*(2), 215–237. https://doi.org/10.1080/00221546.2007.11780874

Miao, F., & Cukurova, M. (2024). *Artificial intelligence (AI) competency framework for teachers.* UNESCO. https://doi.org/10.54675/ZJTE2084

Ng, D. T. K., Leung, J. K. L., Chu, S. K. W., & Qiao, M. S. (2021). Conceptualizing AI literacy: An exploratory review. *Computers and Education: Artificial Intelligence, 2*, Article 100041. https://doi.org/10.1016/j.caeai.2021.100041

Nikitina, S. (2005). Pathways of interdisciplinary cognition. *Cognition and Instruction, 23*(3), 389–425. https://doi.org/10.1207/s1532690xci2303_3

Sperling, K., Stenberg, C.-J., McGrath, C., Åkerfeldt, A., Heintz, F., & Stenliden, L. (2024). In search of artificial intelligence (AI) literacy in teacher education: A scoping review. *Computers and Education Open, 6*, Article 100169. https://doi.org/10.1016/j.caeo.2024.100169

Touretzky, D., Gardner-McCune, C., & Seehorn, D. (2023). Machine learning and the five big ideas in AI. *International Journal of Artificial Intelligence in Education, 33*(2), 233–266. https://doi.org/10.1007/s40593-022-00314-1

Chapter 7
Examining Chinese and American Pre-Service Teachers' Perceptions of AI Ethical Implications

Abstract This exploratory study investigates the shifts in ethical AI perceptions among preservice teachers from the U.S. and China following participation in an AI Literacy for Educators course. Utilizing a pre/post mixed-methods design, the analysis was guided by the FATES framework (fairness, autonomy, transparency, environmental sustainability, and societal impact). Quantitative results revealed one statistically significant shift in environmental sustainability for the U.S. cohort only, with all other dimensions showing non-significant gains for both cohorts. However, triangulation with the qualitative thematic analysis confirmed that the curriculum induced notable affective changes, including patterns of growth, disillusionment, and heightened skepticism, demonstrating that the full impact of ethical education is better captured by thematic evolution than quantitative scales. The most profound finding is a fundamental cultural divergence in where each cohort places responsibility for ensuring ethical AI. The U.S. cohort consistently focused on individual professional duty and financial state intervention, whereas the Chinese cohort prioritized systemic regulatory oversight and educational adaptation. These differences underscore that AI ethics curricula must be culturally responsive, recognizing that the perception of ethical responsibility is mediated by local societal and political frameworks.

7.1 Introduction

In recent years, integrating ethics into AI education has become a core concern of teacher preparation and policy initiatives. Scholars emphasize that ethical literacy requires understanding not only the technical aspects of AI but also its profound societal ramifications (Jobin et al., 2019). To capture the comprehensive nature of these challenges, this study adopts an expanded ethical AI framework built on five critical dimensions: Fairness/Bias, Autonomy/Privacy, Transparency/Explainability, Environmental Sustainability, Societal Impact (FATES). This expanded scope aligns with major global policy mandates recognizing AI's impact across society and the ecosystem (UNESCO, 2021).

I. Lyublinskaya and X. Du, *A Pedagogical Framework for K–12 AI Literacy*, Springer Texts in Education, https://doi.org/10.1007/978-3-032-23570-1_7

Whereas Chap. 6 focused on cognitive gains in AI content knowledge, the present study explores the affective and dispositional outcomes that arise when ethical reasoning is explicitly embedded in AI literacy instruction. This empirical study, which uses a mixed-methods survey, is conducted within the same AI Literacy for Educators course detailed in Chap. 5, involving preservice teachers from both the US and China. The purpose of this exploratory study is to document and explore the shifts in preservice teachers'perceptions about the ethical implications of AI following their participation in the course. Drawing on the Pedagogical Framework for AI Literacy (Chap. 3), ethical reasoning was systematically integrated throughout the course. This integration required preservice teachers to continuously reflect on FATES implications while acquiring AI content knowledge and designing activities to integrate AI literacy into discipline-specific lessons. Beyond documenting shifts in ethical awareness, this chapter also examines how preservice teachers interpret the moral and civic dimensions of AI within their professional roles, positioning AI ethics as a core dimension of pedagogical competence.

7.2 FATES Framework

This FATES Framework comprises five core dimensions and was used as the primary conceptual tool for organizing the analysis of preservice teachers'ethical perceptions regarding AI. This framework extends the canonical fairness, accountability, transparency, and privacy (FATP) principles to incorporate macro-level ethical concerns (environmental and societal impact) that are highly relevant to the civic and professional responsibilities of future educators (UNESCO, 2021).

F: Fairness/Bias

Fairness addresses the ethical imperative that AI systems must produce equitable outcomes, actively mitigating the risk of bias. Algorithmic bias often stems from flawed or non-representative training data, leading to the perpetuation or amplification of existing societal inequities based on demographics like gender, race, or socioeconomic status (Buolamwini & Gebru, 2018). In an educational context, a lack of fairness can manifest in biased grading systems, unequal access to personalized learning resources based on socioeconomic status, or differential identification rates for gifted programs. This dimension focuses on participants' awareness of these risks and the perceived ethical obligation of developers to ensure equity.

A: Autonomy/Privacy

This dimension encompasses the fundamental right to privacy, the protection of personal data and information, and the broader concept of autonomy, which is the individual's ability to maintain control, self-determination, and freedom of choice in an increasingly automated world. As AI takes over high-stakes decision-making, concerns arise about the erosion of human agency and the necessity of retaining human oversight (Floridi, 2019). In education, this includes the ethical management of student data collected by learning management systems, and the need to ensure

AI tutoring systems do not limit student exploration or decision-making autonomy by excessively guiding their learning paths. This dimension captures perceptions regarding the trade-off between AI efficiency and individual control over personal data and life choices.

T: Transparency/Explainability

Transparency, often discussed alongside explainability (XAI), requires that AI systems' functions, decisions, and limitations are clear, auditable, and comprehensible to users and stakeholders. The lack of transparency, the so-called "black box" problem, erodes public trust and prevents accountability when harmful outcomes occur (Weller, 2019). For educators, transparency is crucial for understanding how AI is assessing students, shaping curricula recommendations, or flagging academic integrity violations. This dimension explores how teachers perceive the value of openness for building trust and ensuring the responsible use of AI tools.

E: Environmental Sustainability

Environmental sustainability is a macro-level ethical consideration that assesses AI's ecological footprint. Training and running large AI models require massive computational resources, leading to significant energy consumption and carbon emissions (Patterson et al., 2022). This dimension moves beyond immediate user ethics to examine the global, long-term responsibility of AI actors, including developers and policymakers, to minimize resource depletion and promote sustainable development practices in technology. For instance, this concern addresses the power demands of data centers hosting AI tutoring platforms, the accelerated e-waste cycle from frequent hardware upgrades in school districts, and the high environmental costs associated with streaming and storing massive educational data sets in the cloud.

S: Societal Impact

Societal impact primarily addresses the profound socioeconomic influence of widespread AI automation, most notably concerning mass job displacement and economic disruption (Frey & Osborne, 2017). This dimension requires reflection on the collective, civic responsibility to anticipate and mitigate social upheaval, including the need for new public policies, social safety nets, and educational adaptation strategies to prepare the future workforce for an AI-driven economy. For preservice teachers, this translates into the professional duty to design curriculum that prepares students for jobs that complement, rather than compete with, AI, emphasizing human-centric skills like creativity and emotional intelligence.

7.3 Methodology

This study follows convergent mixed methods survey research design and is guided by the following research questions:

1. To what extent do United States and Chinese preservice teachers'perceptions of AI ethics across the five dimensions of the FATES Framework shift following participation in the course?
2. What emergent themes and conceptual depth regarding ethical obligations and professional responsibility are revealed in the United States and Chinese preservice teachers'perspectives across the five dimensions of the FATES Framework following participation in the course?
3. What are the commonalities and contextual variations in the shifts in ethical perceptions between the United States and Chinese preservice teacher cohorts?

7.3.1 Participants

The initial pool of participants for the AI Literacy for Educators course, which included cohorts from both the United States and China, is described in detail in Chap. 5 (Study Context and Participants). For the purpose of this pre-and post-test survey analysis, only those preservice teachers who provided matched data by completing both the pre-and post-surveys were included in the study sample. The final analytical sample consisted of 52 preservice teachers across both institutions: 28 participants from the U.S. cohort and 24 participants from the Chinese cohort. This matched sample size provides the foundation for the mixed-methods analysis focusing on cohort-specific shifts and subsequent cross-cultural comparison.

7.3.2 Research Instrument

The instrument used for pre-and post-course data collection was a single, adapted mixed-methods survey designed to assess shifts in preservice teachers' perceptions of ethical AI. The instrument was adapted from validated international AI ethics scales and policy frameworks (Jobin et al., 2019; UNESCO, 2021) to specifically align with the five dimensions of the FATES Framework. The Survey consisted of a quantitative component (7 likert-like questions) and a qualitative component (10 open-ended questions)

The seven multiple-choice questions utilized a 5-point Likert scale (1 = Not at all significant/important/concerned to 5 = Extremely significant/important/concerned) to document the strength of participants' ethical perceptions. The ten open-ended questions were included to provide rich conceptual data regarding ethical reasoning, professional responsibility, and solutions to ethical dilemmas. The questions were designed to cover all five dimensions of the FATES framework as shown in Table 7.1.

The FATES Framework served as the a priori codebook for the thematic analysis of the open-ended responses. The framework's five dimensions were operationalized as the major thematic codes. This approach ensured that the qualitative analysis was systematically grounded in the theoretical structure of the study, allowing researchers

Table 7.1 Alignment of survey questions with the dimensions of the FATES framework

FATES dimension	Item No.	Question type	Exact survey item statement
Fairness/bias	Q1	Likert (1–7)	How significant do you think are the issues of fairness and bias in AI systems?
	Q2	Likert (1–7)	How important is it for developers to actively work to eliminate bias and ensure fairness in the AI systems they create?
	Q8	Open-ended	How can the design of an AI system and the data it's trained on impact the fairness of its results, particularly considering examples of bias in AI like predictive policing, image search, or translation tools?
	Q9	Open-ended	Considering the potential for AI bias, what are the ethical obligations of developers in ensuring fairness and mitigating bias in AI systems?
Autonomy/privacy	Q3	Likert (1–7)	How concerned are you about the potential for AI to reduce your individual control and freedom of choice in daily life?
	Q10	Open-ended	As AI takes on more decision-making roles in areas like self-driving cars and medical diagnostics, what potential impacts do you see on individual autonomy and the need for human oversight?
	Q11	Open-ended	What specific limitations, if any, do you believe should be placed on AI systems when they make decisions that directly impact people's lives?
Transparency/Explainability	Q4	Likert (1–7)	How crucial is it for AI systems to be transparent about how they make decisions in order to build trust with users?
	Q12	Open-ended	Considering the impact of AI on individuals and society, what are the ethical obligations of companies to ensure transparency in AI decision-making processes to different stakeholders?
	Q13	Open-ended	How might the lack of transparency in how an AI system makes decisions affect people's willingness to trust and use that system?
Environmental sustainability	Q5	Likert (1–7)	How important do you think it is for AI development to minimize its environmental impact, such as energy consumption and resource use?
	Q14	Open-ended	AI development and deployment have a significant environmental footprint. How can we address AI's environmental footprint to ensure a more sustainable future for AI technologies?

(continued)

Table 7.1 (continued)

FATES dimension	Item No.	Question type	Exact survey item statement
	Q15	Open-ended	What are the ethical responsibilities of developers in creating sustainable AI solutions?
Societal impact	Q6	Likert (1–7)	How concerned are you about the potential for AI-driven automation to cause job displacement and economic disruption across society?
	Q7	Likert (1–7)	How crucial is it for society to anticipate and actively address the potential effects of AI on the economy and job market?
	Q16	Open-ended	How should society address the economic and social challenges of job displacement due to AI-driven automation (e.g., autonomous agents, chatbots)?
	Q17	Open-ended	What specific policies and initiatives should policymakers implement, and how should educational institutions adapt their programs, to effectively prepare the workforce for the changes brought about by AI-driven automation?

to explore emergent themes and conceptual depth within the established ethical domains and ensure alignment between the quantitative and qualitative findings.

7.3.3 Procedure

Data collection for the ethical perceptions survey occurred concurrently with the pedagogical intervention outlined in Chap. 6, ensuring the pre-and post-course assessments accurately bracketed the period of instruction. Participants completed the AI ethics survey twice: a pre-test prior to the first course session and a post-test immediately following the final session.

This procedure was consistent with the content knowledge assessment detailed in Chap. 6, ensuring that the course served as the intervention period for measuring shifts in ethical perception for both groups. All responses were collected online under comparable time constraints. Prior to analysis, all responses were de-identified, and country-level codes were used solely to distinguish cohorts, maintaining participant confidentiality and data integrity on secure institutional servers.

7.3.4 Data Analysis

Data analysis was conducted in a multi-stage process using SPSS 30 and a manual thematic analysis approach to address the three primary research questions regarding shifts in ethical perceptions across the FATES Framework.

To address RQ1: *To what extent do United States and Chinese preservice teachers'perceptions of AI ethics across the five dimensions of the FATES Framework shift following participation in the course?*, quantitative data from the seven Likert-scale items (Q1–Q7) were analyzed separately for each cohort. Descriptive statistics were calculated for the pre-and post-course scores for each of the five FATES dimensions and the total mean score. Scores for each dimension were calculated by averaging the relevant Likert items. To account for the potential interdependence among the five ethical dimensions, a one-way repeated measures Multivariate Analysis of Variance (MANOVA) was performed. This test uses the five FATES dimension scores (fairness, autonomy, transparency, environmental sustainability, and societal impact) as the multiple dependent variables to test for an overall change in the perception profile from pre-to post-course for each cohort. Given the exploratory nature of the study, follow-up paired-samples t-tests were conducted on the aggregated pre- and post-course scores Given the exploratory nature of the study, follow-up paired-samples t-tests were planned to assess specific FATES dimensional shifts.. Effect sizes were calculated using Cohen's d for repeated measures to assess the magnitude of the observed change in each specific dimension, focusing on practical significance in instances where statistical power may have been limited.

To address RQ2: *What emergent themes and conceptual depth regarding ethical obligations and professional responsibility are revealed in the United States and Chinese preservice teachers'perspectives across the five dimensions of the FATES Framework following participation in the course?* qualitative analysis of the 10 open-ended responses (Q8–Q17) was conducted to explore the conceptual depth of preservice teachers'ethical reasoning, focusing on emergent themes and interpretations of professional responsibility. This analysis was performed separately for the U.S. and Chinese cohorts using a manual thematic analysis approach. The FATES Framework served as the a priori thematic codebook, with its five dimensions used as the primary organizing categories. A multi-step process ensured coding rigor:

- Two independent researchers manually read, segmented, and coded all responses, assigning passages to one or more of the five FATES categories.
- Within each FATES dimension, secondary, emergent sub-codes were created inductively to capture nuanced interpretations specific to each cohort.
- To establish inter-rater reliability, 20% of the data was double-coded by the researchers, and inter-rater reliability was calculated using Cohen's Kappa coefficient. A minimum acceptable Kappa value of 0.70 was required before proceeding with the full qualitative dataset analysis.
- Final thematic summaries were generated to document how preservice teachers'ethical interpretations and sense of professional responsibility evolved

across the pre-and post-course survey administrations for each dimension and within each cohort.

To address RQ3: *What are the commonalities and contextual variations in the shifts in ethical perceptions between the United States and Chinese preservice teacher cohorts?* a triangulation strategy (Creswell & Plano Clark, 2018) was employed, synthesizing the quantitative and qualitative findings. Rather than relying solely on direct statistical comparison between groups, we systematically compared the patterns of change identified in RQ1 for each cohort.. The thematic summaries generated separately for the U.S. and Chinese cohorts (from RQ2) were subjected to a constant comparative method. This involved systematically comparing the frequency, depth, and tone of the sub-codes within each FATES dimension to identify shared ethical priorities (commonalities) and culturally mediated interpretations (variations) across the two groups. Finally, the quantitative profiles were integrated with the comparative thematic results. This holistic integration allowed us to answer RQ3 by identifying how cultural context influenced not only the magnitude of ethical shifts (practical significance) but also the specific qualitative nature of the participants' evolving professional responsibility..

7.4 Results

The findings of the empirical study are reported following the order of the research questions outlined in the Methodology. We begin by presenting the descriptive statistics (pre-and post-course means and standard deviations) for the five FATES dimensions across both the U.S. and Chinese cohorts. Next, we address RQ1, reporting the results of the repeated measures MANOVA and follow-up *t*-tests to document statistically significant shifts in ethical perceptions within each national cohort. Following the quantitative results, the emergent themes and conceptual depth derived from the qualitative analysis of the open-ended responses are presented to address RQ2. Finally, the section concludes by addressing RQ3 through the triangulation of quantitative and qualitative findings, illuminating the commonalities and contextual variations in perceptual shifts between the U.S. and Chinese preservice teachers.

7.4.1 Shifts in Ethical Perceptions within U.S. and Chinese Cohorts (RQ1)

The descriptive statistics for the aggregated pre-and post-course scores across the five FATES dimensions and for the total mean scores were computed for both the U.S. ($N = 28$) and Chinese ($N = 24$) cohorts (Table 7.2).

The pre-course data showed an overall high baseline of ethical awareness in both groups, with total mean scores of $M = 4.03$ (U.S.) and $M = 3.81$ (China) on the

Table 7.2 Descriptive statistics for pre-and post-course scores for U.S. and Chinese participants

Survey scores	U.S. ($N = 28$)				China ($N = 24$)			
	M_pre	SD_pre	M_post	SD_post	M_pre	SD_pre	M_post	SD_post
F	4.27	0.80	4.70	0.50	3.94	.71	4.25	0.72
A	3.36	1.13	3.36	1.37	3.04	1.00	3.54	0.83
T	4.18	0.77	4.64	0.56	4.04	0.81	4.29	0.75
E	3.86	0.89	4.46	0.64	3.96	0.86	4.04	0.69
S	4.13	0.81	4.14	0.79	3.91	0.67	3.93	0.68
Total	4.03	0.57	4.31	0.51	3.81	0.51	4.03	0.52

5-point scale. However, critical differences in the pre-course prioritization of ethical dimensions were evident between the national groups.

Prior to the course, the U.S. cohort generally reported higher initial concern across most dimensions. Their highest pre-course score was in Fairness ($M = 4.27$, SD = 0.80), suggesting a strong initial awareness of bias and equity issues. In contrast, the Chinese cohort reported their highest pre-course mean in Transparency ($M = 4.04$, SD = 0.81). The most pronounced divergence was in the Autonomy dimension, where the U.S. cohort showed substantial concern ($M = 3.36$, SD = 1.13), while the Chinese cohort reported a comparatively lower score ($M = 3.04$, SD = 1.00). Both groups exhibited similar moderate pre-course concern regarding the societal impacts of AI (U.S. $M = 4.13$, SD = 0.81; China $M = 3.91$, SD = 0.67).

Following the course intervention, both cohorts showed an overall increase in total mean perception scores (U.S. ΔM = 0.28; China ΔM = 0.22). For the U.S. cohort the greatest post-course mean was observed in the Fairness dimension ($M = 4.70$, SD = 0.50), which remained the highest priority. The most notable increase in concern was for the Environmental Sustainability dimension (ΔM = 0.60), shifting from $M = 3.86$ (SD = 0.89) to $M = 4.46$ (SD = 0.64), suggesting the curriculum strongly impacted this macro-level perception. The Chinese cohort showed the largest internal shift in the Autonomy dimension (ΔM = 0.50) from $M = 3.04$ (SD = 1.00) to $M = 3.54$ (SD = 0.83), significantly closing the initial gap with the U.S. cohort. Perceptions regarding Societal Impact remained relatively stable for both groups (U.S. ΔM = 0.01; China ΔM = 0.02). These descriptive findings suggest that while the course raised overall ethical awareness, the magnitude of the shift was differentially impactful depending on the specific ethical dimension and the national context.

7.4.1.1 The Shifts in the Chinese Cohort

The analysis of the shifts in ethical perceptions for Chinese cohort ($N = 24$) began with a repeated measures MANOVA that treated Time (pre-course/post-course) and the five FATES dimensions (fairness, autonomy, transparency, environmental sustainability, and societal impact) as two within-subjects factors. This analysis

Table 7.3 Results of paired-samples *t*-tests for FATES dimensions (Chinese cohort)

FATES dimension	Mean difference	*t*	*df*	Sig. (two-tailed)	Cohen's *d*
Fairness (F)	0.31	2.532	23	0.019	0.51
Autonomy (A)	0.50	1.928	23	0.062	0.40
Transparency (T)	0.25	1.297	23	0.207	0.26
Environmental sustainability (E)	0.08	0.440	23	0.664	0.09
Societal Impact (S)	0.02	0.127	23	0.900	0.02

confirmed that the five FATES dimensions were perceived as significantly distinct from one another, F(4, 20) = 6.777, $p = 0 .001$ justifying the separate examination of each ethical concept. However, the repeated measures MANOVA did not yield a statistically significant main effect of Time (F(1, 23) = 3.798, $p = 0.064$) or a Time x FATES interaction (F(4, 20) = 1.435, $p = 0.259$). Despite the lack of statistical significance, the large effect size for the interaction ($\eta_p^2 = .223$) suggested a strong practical impact. Consequently, we proceeded to examine dimension-level shifts using paired-samples *t*-tests with Bonferroni correction (α_{adj} =0 .01). These follow-up tests revealed that the course intervention did not result in a statistically significant shift in any of the five ethical dimensions (Table 7.3).

These results suggest that while the curriculum induced notable practical shifts in the Fairness and Autonomyperceptions for the Chinese cohort (indicated by the medium effect sizes), these changes lacked the statistical certainty required to declare them significant under the rigorous Bonferroni criterion.

7.4.1.2 The Shifts in the U.S. Cohort

Similarly, the quantitative analysis for the U.S. cohort ($N = 28$) began with a two-factor repeated measures MANOVA. The test confirmed that preservice teachers perceived the five FATES dimensions as significantly distinct from one another, $F(4, 24) = 7.560, p < 0.001$. However, the overall main effect of Time was not statistically significant, $F(1, 27) = 3.864, p = 0.060$. Furthermore, the Time x FATES interaction was also non-significant, $F(4, 24) = 2.206, p = 0.099$. Despite the lack of statistical significance, the substantial effect size for the interaction ($\eta_p^2 = .269$) suggested a strong practical impact, justifying proceeding with follow-up paired-samples t-tests with the Bonferroni correction ($\alpha_{adj} = 0.01$). These follow-up tests revealed that the course intervention resulted in a statistically significant ($p = 0.02$) shift with a large effect size ($d = 0.66$) in Environmental Sustainability only (Table 7.4).

While shifts in other dimensions did not meet the rigorous adjusted threshold, the dimensions of Transparency and Fairness exhibited medium effect sizes ($d = 0.46$ and d =0 .40, respectively), suggesting meaningful practical shifts in these perceptions.

Table 7.4 Results of paired-samples t-tests for FATES dimensions (the U.S. cohort)

FATES dimension	Mean difference	t	df	Sig. (two-tailed)	Cohen's d
Fairness (F)	0.43	2.121	27	0.043	0.40
Autonomy (A)	0.00	0.000	27	1.000	0.00
Transparency (T)	0.46	2.458	27	0.021	0.46
Environmental sustainability (E)	0.61	3.505	27	0.002	0.66
Societal Impact (S)	0.02	0.083	27	0.935	0.02

7.4.2 *Emergent Themes across FATES (RQ2)*

Thematic analysis was conducted on the 10 open-ended questions (Q8–Q17) provided by the matched participants, analyzing pre-and post-course responses separately for the U.S. and Chinese cohorts. This analysis was guided by the FATES Framework, which served as the a priori coding structure to organize participant interpretations across five key ethical domains. The goal of this analysis was to move beyond the quantitative shifts found in RQ1 to explore the depth, complexity, and sense of professional responsibility embedded in the teachers' own words. The analysis utilized the matched nature of the survey responses to conduct an intra-subject analysis of conceptual change. This approach moved beyond simply tallying thematic frequency to document the specific evolution of ethical complexity within each participant's pre-and post-course narratives, providing a direct link between the curriculum and the shifts in ethical reasoning reported below. The subsequent sections present the pre-to post-course thematic shifts for both the U.S. ($N = 28$) and Chinese ($N = 24$) cohorts, organized by the five FATES dimensions to facilitate cross-cultural comparison.

F: Fairness /Bias

The analysis of the Fairness/Bias dimension revealed an essential difference in the prioritization of mitigation responsibility. Prior to the course, the U.S. cohort primarily attributed bias to "data defects" (i.e., external technical flaws), whereas the Chinese cohort treated fairness as an abstract concept. Post-course, both groups matured in their understanding, but their proposed solutions diverged sharply. U.S. cohort shifted focus to active mitigation and professional duty, emphasizing the educator's specific role in implementing algorithmic auditing and actively testing AI tools for bias against student sub-groups. This demonstrated a strong sense of individual professional responsibility. The dominant theme of the Chinese cohort was the demand for governmental accountability. Chinese preservice teachers advocated for the state to establish legal systems and regulatory oversight to ensure fair algorithm design, placing responsibility on systemic and legal frameworks rather than the individual educator.

A: Autonomy / Privacy

Analysis of the Autonomy/privacy dimension showed a divergence in the perceived threat to individual control. Pre-course, the U.S. preservice teachers feared user dependence leading to intellectual decline, while the Chinese cohort focused on preventing physical risk in systems like autonomous vehicles. In post-course responses, the U.S cohort shifted the emphasis to mandatory human veto and legal liability. U.S. participants strongly advocated for a human-in-the-loop (HIL) system for all high-stakes decisions and demanded clear channels for legal recourse if individual autonomy was compromised by system error. The focus of the Chinese cohort shifted to maintaining human agency and trust within the interface. Chinese participants centered on features that reinforce the user's sense of control, such as a "second confirmation button" to prevent manipulation. Their thematic focus remained on the user's perceived interaction rather than external legal protection.

T: Transparency / Explainability

Both cohorts agreed on the necessity of transparency, but they differed in its function. Post-course thematic analysis showed that the U.S. preservice teachers expected differentiated explainable AI (XAI), such as simplified explanations for non-technical users (parents) but full technical documentation for auditors. Transparency was viewed as a means to ensure functional auditability and governance. Chinese participants framed transparency as a fundamental user right and linked opacity to moral evasion. They argued that companies hide their decision-making processes to "hide their responsibility," viewing transparency as a necessary condition for assigning moral blame and liability.

E: Environmental Sustainability

In alignment with the quantitative findings, both cohorts showed a significant thematic shift in understanding macro-level environmental costs, but their proposed solutions targeted different actors in the AI ecosystem. The strongest post-course theme for the U.S. cohort was external policy demand. U.S. participants advocated for mandatory carbon/water usage reporting for data centers and attention to the e-waste cycle caused by frequent hardware upgrades in schools. The Chinese cohort focused on technological efficiency and green algorithmic design. Chinese participants placed responsibility on developers to prioritize smaller, more efficient models and internal technological solutions to reduce energy demand, placing less emphasis on large-scale governmental regulation.

S: Societal Impact

The two cohorts diverged most sharply on the structural solutions required to mitigate the macroeconomic risk of job displacement. U.S. cohort shifted from passive acceptance to demanding mandated government intervention. Strong emergent themes included advocating for universal basic income and expansive, state-funded retraining programs to create robust social safety nets. The educator's role was defined as teaching non-automatable skills (creativity, empathy). The primary solution suggested by the Chinese cohort was educational adaptation, specifically demanding the integration of AI literacy across all curricula to equip students with necessary skills. They focused on optimizing human capital through educational reform and placed minimal emphasis on state financial safety nets.

Overall, the qualitative analysis revealed a fundamental difference in a way two cohorts viewed ethical responsibility. The U.S. cohort consistently prioritized solutions rooted in professional duty, legal liability, and financial state intervention. In contrast, the Chinese cohort consistently focused on systemic regulatory oversight, maintaining user trust, and optimizing human capital through comprehensive educational reform. While both cohorts achieved conceptual maturity under the FATES Framework, their divergent solutions underscore how cultural and political contexts shape the perception of where ethical accountability should reside, with the individual practitioner and liberal governance (U.S.) or with the governing state and educational system (China). These contrasting thematic priorities form the core of the cross-cultural comparison in the final research question.

7.4.3 *Cross-Cultural Comparison and Triangulation of Perceptual Shifts (RQ3)*

This final research question sought to identify the commonalities and contextual variations in the ethical shifts between the U.S. and Chinese preservice teacher cohorts. To address this, a convergent mixed-methods triangulation was employed, synthesizing the statistical results from the quantitative analysis (RQ1) with the thematic data from the qualitative analysis (RQ2). The goal of this triangulation was to move beyond simply documenting what perceptions changed to explaining how and why those changes differed based on cultural and educational contexts. This section first addresses the commonalities observed across both cohorts and then details the distinct cultural variations in ethical prioritization and proposed solutions, providing a holistic answer to the final research question.

7.4.3.1 Commonalities Across Cohorts

Despite the significant cultural and systemic differences, the analysis revealed two primary commonalities in the impact of the AI literacy course on preservice teachers' perceptions about ethical implications of AI:

- Quantitatively, both the U.S. cohort ($p = 0.043$) and the Chinese cohort ($p = 0.019$) showed the strongest non-significant p-values in the Fairness (F) dimension. While neither met the stringent Bonferroni correction threshold (α_{adj} =0 .01), the low p-values and medium effect sizes (d =0 .40 for the U.S. and d = 0 .51 for China) suggest that the course curriculum on algorithmic bias was the most uniformly impactful subject across both cultures.
- Qualitatively, both cohorts successfully moved from passive and superficial definitions of ethical issues to articulating specific, systemic requirements. By the

post-test, both groups focused on the need for accountability and risk mitigation rather than mere recognition of the ethical challenges.

7.4.3.2 Cultural Variations between Cohorts

Triangulation confirmed that the direction of ethical interpretation and solution-building diverged significantly based on the cohort's contextual frame. This divergence primarily revolved around the perceived role of the individual versus the state in enacting ethical change (Table 7.5).

In summary, the U.S. cohort's response to the ethical challenges was characterized by a critical, rights-based ethos focusing on protection via external governance and safety nets. Conversely, the Chinese cohort's response was characterized by a collectivist, solution-oriented ethos focusing on systemic stability, educational integration, and optimizing human capability within the prevailing technological narrative. These

Table 7.5 Triangulated findings of ethical AI priorities for the U.S. and Chinese preservice teachers

FATES dimension	U.S. cohort (individual/external governance focus)	Chinese cohort (system/human capital focus)
Quantitative shifts (RQ1)	Significant gain in environmental Sustainability ($p = 0.002$, $d = 0.66$). This issue became the highest quantitative priority.	No statistically significant shifts. Strongest practical shifts (medium effect) were in fairness and autonomy.
F: Fairness/bias	Qualitative focus on professional duty and auditing. Mitigation is seen as the individual educator's role (vetting tools, testing bias against student sub-groups).	Qualitative focus on governmental accountability. Mitigation is seen as the state's role (establishing legal systems, regulatory oversight).
A: Autonomy/ privacy	Qualitative focus on legal liability and recourse. Autonomy is preserved by demanding a mandatory human-in-the-loop and clear channels for redress.	Qualitative focus on human agency and trust. Autonomy is preserved by maintaining user control within the interface and preventing cognitive manipulation.
S: Societal impact	Strong qualitative demand for mandated government intervention in the economy, specifically advocating for universal basic income and expansive state-funded social safety nets to protect workers.	Strong qualitative demand for educational adaptation. The primary solution is to integrate AI literacy across all curricula to upgrade human capital and equip students with non-automatable skills. Financial safety nets were rarely mentioned.
E: Environmental sustainability	Qualitative focus on external policy requirements (e.g., mandatory carbon/water usage reporting) to hold data center operators accountable for macro-level impacts.	Qualitative focus on technological efficiency and green design (e.g., using smaller, efficient models) as internal solutions led by developers.

contrasting priorities demonstrate how cultural context mediates the application of ethical AI turning a shared learning experience into divergent policy and professional outlooks.

7.5 Discussion

The purpose of this study was to assess the shifts in preservice teachers'ethical perceptions across the FATES framework dimensions following a completion of an AI Literacy for Educators course and to identify the impact of cultural context on these shifts (RQ3). The findings revealed a complex pattern: the overall lack of statistically significant quantitative change (RQ1) masked profound qualitative and practical changes (RQ2) that diverged sharply along cultural lines, fundamentally changing how the cohorts perceive ethical responsibility. The most salient finding is that ethical education primarily triggered affective and dispositional outcomes rather than uniform shifts on a Likert scale. Analysis of participants' reflections revealed three primary developmental trajectories of change: growth, disillusionment, and resistance.

7.5.1 Affective Outcomes and Trajectories of Change

While both cohorts demonstrated measurable growth in ethical literacy, the direction and affective tone of change was different. On average, Chinese preservice teachers were more likely to report positive shifts, expressing increased confidence, moral clarity, and optimism about AI's ethical use, while the U.S. cohort exhibited a broader spectrum, with a higher proportion of critical or cautious shifts. These contrasting trajectories suggest that ethical reflection elicits different emotional outcomes even when cognitive learning is similar. For many Chinese participants, the curriculum reinforced preexisting narratives of technological progress and moral duty, affirming AI as a socially constructive force when guided by ethical principles. U.S. participants, conversely, often engaged deeply with fairness and privacy dilemmas but left more skeptical of AI's role in education. This divergence mirrors broader contextual distinctions: Chinese teacher education emphasizes collective moral harmony and civic responsibility ("we can ensure AI benefits society"), versus the U.S. focus on individual moral autonomy and critical inquiry. ("I must question and safeguard against bias"). Both outcomes represent growth, but in different moral registers.

The three developmental trajectories explain the complex relationship between knowledge and attitude observed in the quantitative data (RQ1):

- Growth trajectory: This was the dominant trajectory among the Chinese preservice teachers and a significant subset of the U.S. teachers. These participants moved from uncertainty or limited awareness to a more nuanced and positive appreciation

of AI ethics, frequently citing specific learning experiences (e.g., case studies or collaborative discussions) as catalysts. This growth subgroup typically framed lingering concerns as challenges to be managed rather than reasons to reject AI.
- Disillusionment trajectory: This pattern was disproportionately observed among the U.S. cohort. As participants confronted AI's risks and systemic biases, some experienced discomfort or moral fatigue, leading to heightened skepticism. This mirrors the notion of productive struggle, where ethical awareness can initially heighten anxiety before stabilizing into mature judgment. Quantitatively, this trend explains why the U.S. cohort's substantial change in Fairness and Transparency themes only resulted in medium effects ($d = 0.40$), as increased knowledge led to heightened concern rather than increased optimism.
- Reluctance trajectory: A smaller subset in both countries showed stable attitudes, corresponding to a reluctance to change a prior viewpoint. In the U.S., reluctance was tied to a strong critical stance pre-dating the course (confirmation bias), while in China, reluctance was more likely to align with the national rhetoric of AI progress and downplaying ethical issues as distant or solvable.

7.5.2 Cultural Divergence in Ethical Responsibility

The triangulation of the quantitative and qualitative findings (RQ3) reveals that the most profound difference between the cohorts lies in where each cohort places responsibility for ensuring ethical AI (Table 7.5). This pattern highlights that the U.S. cohort views ethical assurance as a mechanism of protection against powerful entities (Big Tech, the government), achieved through individual vigilance and legal liability. Conversely, the Chinese cohort views ethical assurance as a mechanism of system optimization, e.g., problems are solved by mandated regulatory frameworks and enhancing human capital to serve the collective good. The Environmental Sustainability dimension provided the clearest quantitative separation between the cohorts. The U.S. cohort had a statistically significant shift toward environmental concern because their qualitative narrative centered on holding external actors (data centers) accountable through policy demands, a clear rights-based response.

7.6 Implications for AI Ethics Curriculum Design

The findings carry several important implications for designing and implementing AI ethics education in teacher preparation programs:

1. Scaffolding affective outcomes: The presence of the disillusionment trajectory, particularly in the U.S. cohort, suggests that curricula must actively anticipate and manage the emotional impact of confronting systemic risks. Instructors must scaffold learning by introducing success stories and feasible mitigation

strategies immediately after introducing complex dilemmas, ensuring that critical awareness translates into agency and problem-solving rather than skepticism and avoidance.

2. Tailoring cultural frames: Effective AI ethics education must integrate culturally relevant frames. In China, discussions should leverage the concept of collective welfare and social harmony to frame ethical teaching as a contribution to national development. In the U.S., drawing on individual rights, equity, 90, 97, 105, 132, 134 and justice frames is more resonant, focusing on empowering teachers to protect student autonomy and data privacy.
3. Prioritizing the educator's role: The qualitative divergence highlights that curriculum should explicitly address the educator's professional duty within the FATES framework. Teachers must be trained not just to recognize bias, but to understand their role as auditors, curriculum designers focusing on non-automatable human skills, and advocates for ethical policy.

7.7 Conclusions

In conclusion, the findings, analyzed through the expanded FATES Framework, underscore that AI ethics education for preservice teachers must be both pedagogically sound and culture-specific. The study's convergent mixed-methods approach clarified that while the overall course intervention did not produce uniform statistical change on the survey scales (RQ1), it successfully achieved a significant shift in the students' depth of ethical reflection (RQ2), revealing a profound cultural divergence in the application of that ethical knowledge (RQ3). The analysis yielded two critical insights into the learning outcomes:

1. Ethical education generated complex affective changes (growth, disillusionment, resistance), demonstrating that the curriculum's impact is more robustly captured by qualitative thematic analysis (RQ2) than by non-significant quantitative results (RQ1).
2. The most profound difference lies in where each cohort places responsibility for ensuring ethical AI.

We have seen that the same course content can yield divergent outcomes across different groups; thus, a reflexive approach to curriculum design is needed. Educators should strive to scaffold learners' development from whatever their starting point is, actively work to dispel misconceptions or fatalism, and harness cultural values as a bridge to ethical understanding. By doing so, we foster reflective, ethically aware teachers who possess the balanced competence to navigate the promises and perils of AI with a culturally informed and morally grounded perspective. Ultimately, this work contributes to fostering a generation of educators who are prepared to cultivate ethical reasoning and balanced engagement with AI among their own future students.

References

Buolamwini, J., & Gebru, T. (2018). Gender shades: Intersectional *accuracy disparities in commercial gender classification.* In S. A. Friedler & C. Wilson (Eds.), *Proceedings of machine learning research: The 1st conference on fairness, accountability and transparency* (Vol. 81, pp. 77–91). ML Research Press. http://proceedings.mlr.press/v81/buolamwini18a/buolamwini18a.pdf

Creswell, J. W., & Plano Clark, V. L. (2018). *Designing and conducting mixed methods research* (3rd ed.). SAGE.

Floridi, L. (2019). Establishing the rules for building trustworthy AI. *Center for Digital Ethics Research [paper series].* https://doi.org/10.2139/ssrn.3858392

Frey, C. B., & Osborne, M. A. (2017). The future of employment: How susceptible are jobs to computerisation? *Technological Forecasting and Social Change, 114*, 254–280. https://doi.org/10.1016/j.techfore.2016.08.019

Jobin, A., Ienca, M., & Vayena, E. (2019). The global landscape of AI ethics guidelines. *Nature Machine Intelligence, 1*, 389–399. https://doi.org/10.1038/s42256-019-0088-2

Patterson, D., Gonzales, J., Hölzle, U., Le, Q., Liang, C., Munguia, L.-M., Rothchild, D., So, D. R., Texier, M., & Dean, J. (2022). The carbon footprint of machine learning training will plateau, then shrink. *Computer, 55*(7), 18–28. https://doi.org/10.1109/MC.2022.314871

UNESCO. (2021). *Recommendation on the ethics of artificial intelligence.* UNESCO. https://unesdoc.unesco.org/ark:/48223/pf0000381137

Weller, A. (2019). Transparency: Motivations and challenges. In W. Samek, G. Montavon, A. Vedaldi, L. Hansen, & K. R. Müller (Eds.), *Explainable AI: Interpreting, explaining and visualizing deep learning. Lecture notes in computer science* (Vol. 11700, pp. 23–40). Springer. https://doi.org/10.1007/978-3-030-28954-6_2

Chapter 8
Examining AI Literacy Integration in Chinese and American Preservice Teachers' Lesson Plans

Abstract This chapter presents a comparative mixed-methods content analysis of 164 K-12 lesson plans developed by Chinese (N = 104) and American (N = 60) pre-service teachers to integrate AI literacy into subject-specific content. The study assessed the instructional prioritization of AI literacy competencies and the overall depth of integration. The results indicate that a large majority of both cohorts developed interdisciplinary lesson plans integrating AI literacy as an integral part of disciplinary inquiry, thus establishing a shared pedagogical baseline. However, analysis of the instructional prioritization of AI literacy competencies indicated a strategic divergence in instructional goals. The Chinese cohort viewed AI literacy as the core mechanism for methodological mastery and technical application to solve real-world problems. Conversely, the American cohort viewed AI as a powerful tool for critical oversight and ethical critique. These findings validate two distinct yet effective models for AI literacy fusion, providing essential evidence for tailoring future global teacher preparation programs to specific instructional outcomes.

8.1 Introduction

This chapter builds directly upon the empirical findings of the preceding chapters, which established the influence of the AI literacy course on Chinese and American participants' AI competence and ethical reasoning. In this chapter we pivot to the practical dimension of pedagogical practice. For each cohort we examine two core aspects of this translational process: first, the AI literacy competencies defined by our Pedagogical Framework for AI Literacy (see Chap. 3) that pre-service teachers chose to prioritize and integrate within K-12 disciplines; and second, the levels of AI literacy integration achieved, moving beyond mere technological awareness to assess whether AI is used as an integral methodology or a transformative element within the discipline. Through a comparative mixed methods content analysis, this chapter provides an assessment of the course impact on instructional planning and suggests how cultural and philosophical differences might have shaped the practical tasks prepared by Chinese and American participants for K–12 students.

I. Lyublinskaya and X. Du, *A Pedagogical Framework for K–12 AI Literacy*, Springer Texts in Education, https://doi.org/10.1007/978-3-032-23570-1_8

8.2 Analytical Frameworks

The systematic analysis is built upon theoretical models established in earlier chapters, providing the structured criteria necessary for comparative content analysis. The following sections detail the tools and structured templates utilized to analyze the lesson plans.

8.2.1 AI Literacy Competencies, Learning Outcomes, and Thematic Focus

The codebook for the coding of AI literacy goals within the lesson plans was based directly on the Pedagogical Framework for AI Literacy (see Chap. 3) that established six core AI literacy competencies and associated student learning outcomes for each component of the framework. (Table 8.1).

This codebook was used to track the frequency and thematic priorities of AI literacy concepts embedded in the lesson plans developed by the Chinese and American participants.

Table 8.1 Codebook for AI literacy competency qualitative analysis

Component	Code	Focus of analysis	Learning outcome focus
Design	D1	Problem framing, idea generation	Initial design process, empathetic understanding, defining authentic problems, generating innovative ideas
	D2	Critical evaluation of AI applications	Critical evaluation of AI technologies, assessing effectiveness, accuracy, perspective, and credibility
Create	C1	Hands-on prototyping/testing	Transforming ideas into tangible prototypes, systematic testing, analyzing results, and iterating
	C2	Collaborative design and ethical responsibility	Co-design and peer review, collaborative evaluation of the fairness, social relevance, and human impact of solutions
Reflect	R1	Metacognition and ethical self-assessment	Evaluating the success, ethical trade-offs, unforeseen societal impacts of solutions, design choices, and data bias
	R2	Informing future design and digital agency	Actionable revisions to solutions, formulating principles for responsible innovation, demonstrating digital agency

8.2.2 Levels of AI Literacy Integration Framework

The depth of AI literacy integration for each lesson plan was assessed using a five-level ordinal scale framework (Table 8.2), which was developed for this study. This scale is grounded in two established frameworks:

1. The Substitution, Augmentation, Modification and Redefinition (SAMR) four-level model for technology integration (Puentedura, 2013), which informs the progression of technology integration from a simple tool to the transformation of the discipline.
2. A four-level model spanning from intradisciplinary to transdisciplinary reflecting the scope of disciplinary integration (Drake & Reid, 2018).

This scale was the basis for the quantitative scoring of the entire dataset.

8.3 Methodology

This study employs a mixed methods comparative content analysis and is guided by the following research questions:

1. What AI literacy competencies are prioritized in the lesson plans developed by the pre-service teachers, and how does that compare between the Chinese and American cohorts?
2. What is the overall distribution of AI literacy integration levels in the lesson plans developed by the pre-service teachers and how does that compare between the Chinese and American cohorts?
3. What distinct pedagogical traditions are revealed by the intersection of prioritized AI literacy competencies and achieved integration levels in the lesson plans developed by the Chinese and American participants across disciplinary contexts?

8.3.1 Data Collection and Analysis

All data were collected from participants using a standardized Planning Template for AI Literacy Integration described in Chap. 4. This template, developed based on the Understanding by Design (UbD) backward design model (Wiggins et al., 2005), required pre-service teachers to explicitly articulate the connection between: the subject-specific content standards and AI literacy learning outcomes within the five stages of design-thinking process, ensuring that the integration was systematic rather than incidental.

The data set comprised a total of 164 lesson plans developed by pre-service teachers across various K-12 subjects, ranging from elementary art and mathematics

Table 8.2 Quantitative rating form for the levels of AI Literacy Integration and alignment with accepted frameworks

Level	Description and indicators	SAMR equivalent	Disciplinary integration level
0	No integration	None	None
	AI literacy concepts are entirely absent from the lesson plan. The discipline is taught in isolation from any AI-related knowledge or discussion		
	Indicators: No mention of AI concepts, principles, societal impacts, or ethical considerations. The lesson plan does not include learning about AI. The lesson might integrate AI tools, but not learning about AI		
1	AI literacy as an isolated topic / awareness	Substitution	Intradisciplinary (internal, confined within a single discipline)
	AI literacy concepts are introduced as a separate, distinct topic or a brief add-on, largely decoupled from the main disciplinary content. Students might learn about AI in a general sense, but it's not explicitly or deeply connected to the discipline's specific learning objectives or content		
	Indicators: • A dedicated "What is AI?" segment or lecture that is presented as general knowledge, without explicit links to the discipline's specific subject matter • A brief discussion of AI's general ethical implications (e.g., privacy, bias) that lacks specific disciplinary examples or applications • Lesson plans include a single reading about AI, but follow-up activities do not require the integration of this knowledge into the subject matter • Learning objectives related to AI are generic and standalone		
2	AI literacy as a contextual lens for disciplinary understanding	Augmentation	Multidisciplinary (additive, bringing disciplines together without merging them)
	AI literacy concepts are used to provide context or a new lens for understanding specific content or issues within the discipline. The discipline's content becomes a case study or a framework for discussing AI, or vice versa. The focus is on making explicit connections		

(continued)

Table 8.2 (continued)

Level	Description and indicators	SAMR equivalent	Disciplinary integration level
	Indicators: • The lesson plan explicitly prompts students to consider how AI principles (e.g., data analysis, algorithmic decision-making, pattern recognition) relate to or influence core concepts within the discipline • Activities require students to examine disciplinary phenomena through an AI lens, or to understand AI's impact on a disciplinary context • Discussions or assignments require students to draw parallels between disciplinary methods/theories and AI concepts • Learning objectives connect AI concepts to disciplinary understanding at a foundational level		
3	AI literacy as an integral part of disciplinary inquiry/critical application	Modification	Interdisciplinary (fusion, true blending of subjects to create a new, integrated understanding)
	AI literacy concepts are deeply integrated into the discipline's core inquiry processes, critical thinking, or problem-solving. Students are expected to use their understanding of AI to critically analyze, evaluate, or propose solutions to disciplinary problems, with the discipline serving as the rich context for this critical AI engagement		
	Indicators: • Students are required to critically evaluate disciplinary content, methods, or outcomes by applying their knowledge of AI's capabilities, limitations, and ethical dimensions • Assignments demand that students synthesize disciplinary knowledge with AI literacy to address complex problems or questions • The lesson plan poses authentic, complex disciplinary challenges where an understanding of AI literacy is essential to developing sophisticated responses or analyses • Learning objectives require higher-order thinking skills where AI literacy is crucial for achieving deep disciplinary understanding and problem-solving		

(continued)

Table 8.2 (continued)

Level	Description and indicators	SAMR equivalent	Disciplinary integration level
4	AI literacy as a transformative element in redefining disciplinary boundaries / transdisciplinary reflection	Redefinition	Transdisciplinary (non-disciplinary, conceptual structure that is no longer strictly bound by the original disciplines)
	AI literacy concepts are used to explore how AI fundamentally reshapes or even redefines the discipline itself, its methodologies, its core questions, or its future. Students engage in highly complex, abstract, or forward-looking discussions about the nature of knowledge, human roles, and the future of the discipline in an AI-infused world. This often involves questioning traditional disciplinary boundaries due to AI's influence		
	Indicators: • The lesson plan encourages students to theorize about the future evolution of the discipline in an AI-permeated world, considering how AI might alter its foundational principles, research questions, or professional practices • Students are prompted to critically re-examine the very nature of knowledge, creativity, or decision-making within the discipline in light of advanced AI • Assignments involve conceptual design or visionary thinking about how AI could lead to entirely new sub-fields, methodologies, or ethical considerations within or across disciplines • Learning objectives push students to engage with philosophical or meta-level questions about the discipline's identity and boundaries in an AI-rich context		

to high school physics, history, and algebra. The Chinese dataset included 104 lesson plans submitted by 26 students, each submitting four plans. The US dataset included 60 lesson plans submitted by 16 students, with submissions ranging from three to five plans per student. This collection of lesson plans was previously utilized and described in Chap. 4 for the formal validation of the Pedagogical Framework for AI Literacy, and is now being analyzed to address the study research questions.

The analysis followed a systematic three-step procedure:

Step 1: Content analysis to explore prioritization of AI literacy competencies:

- The content of each lesson plan was analyzed using the AI literacy competencies codebook (Table 8.1). A competency was coded as present if the lesson explicitly required students to engage in the corresponding behavior (e.g., debating ethical trade-offs for R1, or creating a labeled dataset for C1). The statistical results from this presence/absence coding were then interpreted through a subsequent qualitative thematic analysis, focusing on the distinct instructional goals for the competencies. It is noteworthy that the presence/absence data for these AI literacy competencies were originally collected and used in Chap. 4 to establish construct validity of the DCR cycle of the Pedagogical Framework for AI Literacy, and are reused here for comparative content analysis of instructional priorities.
- Descriptive statistics, including raw frequencies and relative percentages of appearance for each competency were then calculated separately for the Chinese and American cohorts.
- Chi-square tests were used to compare the frequency of each competency across the two cohorts. This analysis determined whether statistically significant differences in the prioritization of competencies exist between the Chinese and American participants.

Step 2: Analysis of AI literacy integration levels:

- The overall instructional strategy of each lesson was rated using the Levels of AI Literacy Integration Framework (Table 8.2).
- Prior to final scoring, inter-rater reliability was established using a randomly selected subset of lessons ($n = 25$, 15%) coded independently by two researchers. The intraclass correlation coefficient was calculated to ensure consistency of the ordinal ratings (Levels 0–4).
- The frequency distribution of integration scores (Levels 0–4) was then calculated for each national cohort.
- To determine whether statistically significant differences exist in the AI literacy integration levels between the Chinese and American cohorts, the Mann–Whitney U Test was used to compare the median rankings of integration scores (Levels 0–4) between the two groups.

Step 3: Comparative analysis and synthesis:

- The competency codes and integration scores were combined.
- The thematic patterns (derived from Step 1) and the statistical differences (derived from Step 2) were synthesized to articulate the distinct pedagogical traditions revealed by the intersection of prioritized competencies and integration levels across disciplinary contexts.

8.4 Results

The presentation of results is organized into three main sections according to the research questions: the thematic prioritization of AI literacy competencies (RQ1), the comparative distribution of AI literacy integration levels (RQ2), and a final synthesis of these findings to articulate distinct pedagogical traditions (RQ3).

8.4.1 Prioritization of AI Literacy Competencies (RQ1)

The frequency analysis confirms that both cohorts overwhelmingly prioritized D2 (Critical evaluation of AI applications) and C1 (Prototyping and testing solutions) for K-12 students. However, a significant divergence in instructional focus was identified, establishing two distinct pedagogical goals: the Chinese lesson plans showed a significantly stronger emphasis on problem framing (D1) and collaborative application (C2), while the American lesson plans placed a significantly stronger emphasis on individual digital agency (R2).

8.4.1.1 *Analysis of Competencies in Chinese Lesson Plans*

The Chinese lesson plans ($N = 104$) revealed a commitment to a holistic AI literacy approach, with five out of six competencies present in over three-quarters of the lessons. This breadth suggests a pedagogical goal of linking foundational technical skills to practical societal application. The cohort's instructional ambition is best characterized by the Actionable Design for Disciplinary Mastery, positioning students as active creators and ethical auditors of AI systems used to solve real-world problems. The frequency breakdown, including the thematic focus derived from the qualitative analysis, is detailed in Table 8.3.

The frequencies presented in Table 8.3 demonstrate a purposeful instructional flow that starts with problem definition and culminates in collaborative application:

- Foundational technical core (C1 and D2): The universal pairing of C1 (97.1%) and D2 (96.2%) establishes that AI literacy begins with K-12 students building a model (the prototype) to ground their critical evaluation of AI applications (D2).
- Defining priorities in problem framing (D1) and application (C2): The high frequencies of both D1 (68.3%) and C2 (76.0%) reflect the cohort's emphasis on the full design cycle. D1 prioritizes teaching students to translate complex societal issues into solvable problems, and C2 requires students to apply AI concepts to develop disciplinary knowledge and solve real-world problems through teamwork. This suggests a pedagogical goal of preparing students for communal innovation and systemic problem-solving.

Table 8.3 Frequency and percentage distribution of AI literacy competencies in Chinese lessons ($N = 104$)

Competency	Frequency	Percentage	Key thematic focus
C1 (Prototyping & testing solutions)	101	97.1%	Developing disciplinary knowledge through modeling
D2 (Critically evaluating AI applications)	100	96.2%	AI as a vehicle for disciplinary critique
R2 (Informing future design and digital agency)	81	77.9%	Proposing governance and transparency
C2 (Collaborative design and ethical responsibility)	79	76.0%	Applying AI concepts to develop disciplinary knowledge
R1 (Metacognitive and ethical self-assessment)	79	76.0%	Contrasting human and algorithmic processes
D1 (Problem framing and idea generation)	71	68.3%	Translating civic and disciplinary problems into AI logic

- Integrated reflection (R1 and R2): Both R1 and R2 are integrated into over three-quarters of the lessons, ensuring that ethical reflection (R1: contrasting human vs. algorithmic processes) is tightly coupled with the practical application tasks (C2).

8.4.1.2 *Analysis of Competencies in American Lesson Plans*

The American lesson plans ($N = 60$) showed a highly concentrated instructional focus, with C1, R2, and D2 forming a core cluster dedicated to developing students' technical literacy and their individual responsibility in managing AI outputs. This approach is characterized by *Personalized Reflection and Proactive Digital Citizenship,* centering on individual competence and autonomy within the AI ecosystem. The frequency breakdown and the corresponding thematic focus derived from the qualitative analysis are detailed in Revised Table 8.4.

The analysis of Table 8.4 shows a distinct instructional priority:

- Foundational technical core (C1 and D2): The high frequency of C1 (98.3%) and D2 (86.7%) demonstrates that the AI literacy course instilled a pedagogical emphasis on hands-on design followed by critical evaluation.
- Defining priority in digital agency (R2): The highest-frequency reflection competency is R2 (91.7%), reflecting a core instructional priority that centers on the individual student's competence in exercising proactive digital citizenship. The thematic focus is on students proposing governance and transparency for ubiquitous AI systems (e.g., social media algorithms).
- De-emphasis of initial framing and collaboration: The significantly lower frequencies for D1 (50.0%) and C2 (53.3%) suggest the instructional design bypasses the

Table 8.4 Frequency and percentage distribution of AI literacy competencies in American lesson plans ($N = 60$)

Competency	Frequency	Percentage	Key thematic focus
C1 (Prototyping & testing solutions)	59	98.3%	Developing disciplinary knowledge through modeling
R2 (Informing future design and digital agency)	55	91.7%	Proposing governance and transparency
D2 (Critically evaluating AI applications)	52	86.7%	AI as a vehicle for disciplinary critique
R1 (Metacognitive and ethical self-assessment)	37	61.7%	Contrasting human and algorithmic processes
C2 (Collaborative design and ethical responsibility)	32	53.3%	Applying AI concepts to develop disciplinary knowledge
D1 (Problem framing and idea generation)	30	50.0%	Translating civic and disciplinary problems into AI logic

initial stage of independent problem framing and places less priority on collaboration, centering the instructional effort more on the individual's role in the AI ecosystem.

8.4.1.3 *Comparative Analysis of Competencies*

The Pearson χ^2 test was applied to all six competencies to identify statistically significant differences in instructional priorities between the Chinese and American cohorts. The analysis confirms a divergence rooted in the initial design (D1), collaboration (C2), and individual reflection (R2) (Table 8.5).

The χ^2 test reveals four statistically significant differences in instructional priorities:

- Problem framing (D1): The difference in D1 was statistically significant ($\chi^2(1) = 5.368$, $p = 0.021$), with the Chinese cohort exhibiting a significantly higher instructional priority (68.3% vs. 50.0% for the US cohort). This supports the Chinese cohort's focus on actionable design, requiring students to engage with the design cycle from its conceptual beginning by translating civic and disciplinary problems into solvable AI logic.
- Critically evaluating AI applications (D2): The difference was statistically significant ($\chi^2(1) = 5.050$, $p = 0.025$), with the Chinese cohort showing a significantly higher priority (96.20% vs. 86.70%). However, given the high instructional frequency in both cohorts, this competency is better characterized as a shared core technical focus for both groups, as stated above. The statistical difference confirms a stronger emphasis in the Chinese plans, but the near-universal inclusion in both cohorts validates it as an instructional baseline.

Table 8.5 Statistical and thematic comparison of AI literacy competencies in Chinese and American lesson plans

Competency	China	US	χ^2	Sig.(p)	Thematic distinction
D1 (Problem framing)	68.30%	50.00%	5.368	.021	Chinese participants prioritized translating complex civic problems into AI logic
D2 (Critically evaluating)	96.20%	86.70%	5.050	.025	Chinese participants prioritized the critical evaluation of AI applications significantly higher (shared core technical focus)
C1 (Prototyping & testing)	97.10%	98.30%	.237	.626	No significant difference (core instructional approach)
C2 (Collaborative design)	76.00%	53.30%	8.907	.003	Chinese participants prioritized applying AI to develop disciplinary knowledge and solve real-world problems
R1 (Metacognitive & ethical)	76.00%	61.70%	3.756	.053	No significant difference (core instructional approach)
R2 (Digital agency)	77.90%	91.70%	5.105	0.024	US participants prioritized proposing governance and exercising proactive digital citizenship

- Collaborative design and ethical responsibility (C2): The difference was highly significant ($\chi^2(1) = 8.907$, $p = 0.003$), with the Chinese cohort showing a substantially higher priority (76.0% vs. 53.3%). This confirms that the Chinese pedagogical goal is focused on communal application and the development of disciplinary knowledge through collaborative design projects.
- Informing future design and digital agency (R2): The difference was statistically significant ($\chi^2(1) = 5.105$, $p = 0.024$), with the American cohort showing a higher instructional priority (91.7% vs. 77.9% for the Chinese cohort). This confirms the American cohort's focus on proactive digital citizenship, specifically teaching students to formulate and propose governance principles for AI systems they encounter in daily life.

In summary, the data reveals that while both cohorts share a core technical focus (C1 and D2), the Chinese cohort defines AI literacy as a collaborative, design-oriented process leading to systemic solutions (D1 and C2), whereas the American cohort defines it as a concentrated, individual process leading to proactive digital agency and personal responsibility (R2).

8.4.2 Analysis of AI Literacy Integration Levels (RQ2)

Analysis of lesson plans developed by Chinese participants demonstrated a highly integrated approach, with the majority of instruction dedicated to the higher levels of AI literacy integration. The data show that nearly three-quarters of the lesson plans exhibited AI literacy integration at Level 3 (72.1%), where AI serves as the core methodological tool requiring merging AI concepts and disciplinary content for mastering specific subject matter. An additional 22.1% of plans achieved Level 2, where AI literacy provides a contextual lens; however, this level is characterized by an additive approach rather than deep synthesis. The highest level, Level 4, was present in 1.9% of the sample, showcasing a select few instances of using AI literacy to question foundational disciplinary principles. Notably, only 3.8% of the plans scored at Level 1, and Level 0 was entirely absent. (Table 8.6). This distribution, with 94.2% of lesson plans scoring at Level 2 or higher and the overwhelming majority of lessons at Level 3 underscores a systemic commitment of the Chinese cohort to meaningfully embedding AI literacy within disciplinary instruction.

The lesson plans developed by the American participants exhibited a profile defined by consistency and a strong inclination toward advanced integration. The data show a high commitment to embedding AI literacy, with 93.3% of all plans scoring at Level 2 or higher. The dominant mode of integration was Level 3, which was present in 70% of the lesson plans. This majority demonstrates the deep methodological embedding of AI literacy, where concepts are utilized to create a genuine fusion of AI concepts with disciplinary content. An additional 23.3% of plans achieved Level 2, where AI literacy provided a contextual, but non-integrated, lens. Level 4 was present in 3.3% of the plans showcasing rare instances that challenged fundamental disciplinary boundaries. Finally, the American cohort exhibited minimal scores at the lowest integration level, with only 3.3% of plans scoring at Level 1, and the complete absence of Level 0. (Table 8.7) This pattern indicates that instructional effort is overwhelmingly focused on achieving the synthesis required by the higher integration levels.

The high consistency of the scoring, validated by a strong inter-rater reliability (established via Intraclass Correlation Coefficient (ICC > .8 on a subset of 25

Table 8.6 Frequency and percentage distribution of integration levels in Chinese lesson plans ($N = 104$)

Integration level	Frequency	Percentage%
4 (Transformative)	2	3.8
3 (Integral)	75	72.1
2 (Contextual)	23	22.1
1 (Isolated)	4	1.9

Table 8.7 Frequency and percentage distribution of integration levels in America lesson plans ($N = 60$)

Integration level	Frequency	Percentage%
4 (Transformative)	2	3.3
3 (Integral)	42	70
2 (Contextual)	14	23.3
1	2	3.3

randomly selected lessons), affirms the fidelity of the overall scoring. The Mann–Whitney U test was then conducted to compare the distribution of AI literacy integration scores (Levels 0–4) between the Chinese (N = 104) and American (N = 60) lesson plans. The analysis revealed no statistically significant difference in the ranking of integration scores between the two cohorts, U = 3104, $p = .945$). The descriptive data showed the mean ranks of the two cohorts were practically the same (MR = 82.35 for Chinese cohort and MR = 82.77 for the American cohort. This lack of statistical significance suggests a shared pedagogical baseline and ceiling in terms of overall integration capacity. Both groups achieved a common instructional goal by consistently using AI literacy as a core methodological tool with Level 3 being the dominant integration level for both cohorts. This confirms that the thematic divergences identified in competency priorities, specifically in problem framing (D1) and collaborative design (C2), are not the result of differing capacities for integration, but rather a matter of prioritization within this shared high-level capacity for fusion. Both cohorts can achieve deep integration, but they apply that capacity to different educational objectives.

8.4.3 Synthesis of Findings: Revealing Distinct Pedagogical Traditions (RQ3)

Further thematic comparison indicated that both cohorts shared a strong pedagogical priority for AI concepts to be central to the learning objective. However, the instructional design to support this priority was different for each cohort, reflecting their dominant subject areas and professional training. The Chinese participants demonstrated a significantly greater concentration on embedding AI as the core, active methodology for achieving disciplinary content mastery (supported by high rates in D1 and C2). Their lessons rigorously pushed students toward hands-on design, prototyping, and collaborative application to demonstrate deep understanding of the existing curriculum structure. On the contrary, the American participants primarily used AI as a critical and ethical lens, focusing instructional energy on evaluative and policy-making skills (supported by a significantly higher rate in R2). Their lessons consistently required students to propose governance principles and engage in meta-level reflection that challenges the societal identity and real-world application of the discipline in an AI-permeated world. (Table 8.8).

Table 8.8 Side-by-side comparison of pedagogical traditions between the Chinese and the American cohorts

Analytical dimension	Chinese pedagogical tradition	American pedagogical tradition
Intersection of data	The strategic priority on problem framing (D1, 68.3%) and collaborative design (C2, 76.0%) confirms a focus on active system building. This capacity is applied within the context of a high overall integration capacity (Level 3 dominant, 81.7%)	The strategic priority on digital agency (R2, 91.7%) and critical evaluation (D2, 86.7%) confirms a focus on ethical oversight. This capacity is applied within the context of a high overall integration capacity (Level 3 dominant, 65.0%)
Instructional goals	To achieve indispensable mastery through creation. AI is the active tool used to codify, build, and verify the disciplinary concept (e.g., translating a concept into a functional prototype)	To achieve critical oversight through governance. AI is the ethical lens used to critique the societal impact of the discipline and formulate policy proposals
Disciplinary alignment	AI literacy is used to proactively build a better social solution and challenge the cultural neutrality of technology by applying concepts to soft fields (e.g., using AI design to preserve cultural heritage)	AI literacy is used to reinforce the structural integrity of the existing disciplinary framework by applying concepts to rigorous logic (e.g., using algebraic functions to precisely model an algorithm)

In summary, the statistical stability in overall integration scores confirms a shared pedagogical baseline and high capacity in integration of AI literacy (Level 3) in both cohorts. This means the proven divergence in competency priorities (D1, C2, and R2) is not the result of differing capacities for deep integration, but rather a matter of strategic prioritization: The Chinese tradition uses AI literacy as the core mechanism for methodological mastery and application (D1 and C2), while the American tradition targets critical oversight and policy-making (R2). Both groups succeed, but they apply that shared capacity to fundamentally different educational objectives.

8.5 Discussion

The synthesis of findings suggests the existence of two effective, but distinct pedagogical traditions guiding the integration of AI literacy into teaching and learning, providing empirical evidence that instructional intent is most likely shaped by an educational culture. The stability of the overall integration capacity suggests both cohorts achieved a shared methodological baseline, but applied this capacity to divergent educational objectives.

The Chinese pedagogical tradition demonstrated a statistically significant priority for methodological mastery and system creation (D1, problem framing, and C2, collaborative design). This tradition views AI literacy as the core mechanism for rigorous application, where ethical responsibility is integrated into the design process to successfully codify, build, and verify disciplinary knowledge. On the contrary, the American tradition demonstrated a statistically significant priority for critical oversight and policy-making (R2, digital agency). This approach positions AI literacy as the critical and ethical lens for evaluation, where the core teaching priority is to prepare students to challenge the societal and ethical application of autonomous systems and propose governance principles for the knowledge they learn.

8.6 Conclusions

This chapter presented a mixed-methods analysis of pre-service teachers' lesson plans to integrate AI literacy into subject-specific content. The results confirm that both the Chinese and American cohorts have successfully moved past superficial integration, with 73.8% of all lesson plans achieving deep fusion of AI literacy and disciplinary content (Level 3 or 4). However, the statistical analysis also confirmed a difference in instructional priorities that define two distinct pedagogical traditions.

The Chinese cohort of preservice teachers, whole lessons were primarily rooted in Humanities context and whose members largely came from Undergraduate/Masters programs, prioritized D1 (problem framing) and C2 (collaborative design). They viewed AI as the core mechanism for methodological mastery and technical application to solve real-world problems. This pedagogical tradition uses AI literacy to solidify the existing curriculum's rigorous structure by demanding students build and verify concepts.

Conversely, the American cohort of pre-service teachers, whose lessons were overwhelmingly taught within STEM contexts and whose members largely came from Masters/Doctoral programs with extensive K-12/College teaching experience, prioritized R2 (digital agency). They viewed AI as a powerful tool for critical oversight and ethical critique. This tradition uses AI literacy to challenge the discipline's identity by pushing for meta-level reflection and the proactive proposal of governance principles.

The study also validates two effective models for AI literacy integration while highlighting a needed synthesis for global AI literacy teacher training:

- The successful high-frequency model of Level 3 integration observed in both cohorts should be adopted globally to ensure ethical and societal critiques are rooted in actual algorithmic literacy. Students must know how the AI makes a decision before they can critique its fairness.
- Teacher preparation programs aiming for holistic AI literacy must intentionally bridge the gap between technical mastery (the Chinese cohort's priority) and systemic critique (the American cohort's priority). Future curriculum design could integrate reflection prompts (e.g., "How does AI redefine authorship?") into technical curricula hands-on design tasks into ethical curricula.

- These findings provide the essential evidence for designing future teacher preparation programs based not just on the overall capacity for integration, but on the explicit pedagogical goals and cultural outcomes desired by each cohort's educational context. Teacher training policy should distinguish between the competencies needed for methodological verification (D1/C2) and those needed for systemic critique (R2), training teachers in both methodologies rather than assuming competency in one area automatically leads to instructional ambition in the other.

These findings provide the essential evidence for designing future teacher preparation programs based not just on competence, but on the explicit pedagogical goals of different educational cultures.

References

Drake, S. M., & Reid, L. J. (2018) Integrated curriculum as an effective way to teach 21st century capabilities. *Asia Pacific Journal of Educational Research, 1*(1), 31–50. https://doi.org/10.30777/apjer.2018.1.1.03

Puentedura, R. R. (2013, May 29). *SAMR: Moving from enhancement to transformation* [Web log post]. http://www.hippasus.com/rrpweblog/archives/000095.html

Wiggins, G., & McTighe, J. (2005). *Understanding by Design* (Expanded 2nd ed.). Association for Supervision and Curriculum Development.

Chapter 9
Synthesis of Findings and Implications for AI Literacy in Teacher Education

Abstract This chapter synthesizes the empirical findings from a comparative study on the effectiveness of an AI Literacy for Educators course delivered to pre-service teachers in the United States and China. The analysis sought to understand how the pedagogical intervention influenced gains across three dimensions: AI content knowledge, ethical reasoning, and instructional design capacity. Findings suggest the intervention was universally effective, fostering significant improvements in knowledge and a shared high capacity for deep AI literacy integration, which supports the structural integrity of the instructional model (Five Big Ideas in AI and DCR cycle). However, the study indicates that the enactment of AI literacy is a culturally situated construct. While both cohorts achieved a shared high capacity, they developed distinct pedagogical profiles based on their instructional goals for students: U.S. participants prioritized critical oversight, emphasizing digital agency and ethical critique. Conversely, Chinese participants favored methodological mastery, focusing on collaborative design and problem framing. This divergence is linked to differences in cultural framings of moral agency and distinct national pedagogical traditions. The chapter concludes by offering policy and program recommendations, emphasizing the need to institutionalize AI literacy as a pedagogical foundation in teacher preparation programs, utilizing the Pedagogical Framework for AI Literacy as an empirically supported instructional design model for AI literacy integration in K-12 education.

9.1 Introduction

This chapter synthesizes the empirical insights from Chaps 5 through 8 to construct a holistic understanding of how pre-service teachers in the United States and China develop, integrate, and reflect upon AI literacy through the Pedagogical Framework for AI Literacy. Together, these preceding chapters provide converging evidence that AI literacy is not a static skill set but a developmental and culturally mediated process—one in which conceptual, ethical, and practical competencies evolve through scaffolded experiences that bridge technical fluency with reflective inquiry. The findings demonstrate that AI literacy education, when structured around

I. Lyublinskaya and X. Du, *A Pedagogical Framework for K–12 AI Literacy*, Springer Texts in Education, https://doi.org/10.1007/978-3-032-23570-1_9

the Design–Create–Reflect (DCR) cycle, can meaningfully transform pre-service teachers' understanding of AI and their pedagogical capacity to guide students in an AI-shaped world.

The synthesis presented here integrates three core dimensions of teacher learning:

1. Conceptual and cognitive gains (Chapter 6): This dimension addresses the extent of improvement in AI content knowledge and how those learning gains varied across the Five Big Ideas in AI (Perception, Representation & Reasoning, Learning, Natural Interaction, and Societal Impact). The key inquiry was identifying significant differences in comparative gains between the two national contexts.
2. Ethical and dispositional growth (Chapter 7): This dimension explores pre-service teachers' perceptions of AI ethics and how their ethical awareness shifted following the course, particularly within the five dimensions of the FATES Framework. The focus here is on identifying commonalities and contextual variations in ethical reasoning between the Chinese and American cohorts.
3. Pedagogical enactment (Chapter 8): This applied dimension analyzes the lesson plans developed by participants, addressing which AI literacy competencies are prioritized and the overall distribution of AI literacy integration levels. The synthesis reveals how distinct pedagogical traditions intersect with AI integration goals across the two countries.

Taken together, these three dimensions illustrate how AI literacy emerges as a multidimensional construct spanning cognition, ethics, and practice, while also revealing cross-cultural variations in instructional goals and design, interpretation, agency, and responsibility.

Across both countries, pre-service teachers entered the course with limited prior exposure to artificial intelligence concepts but with strong curiosity and a growing awareness of AI's societal relevance. By the end of the program, they demonstrated measurable gains in conceptual understanding and ethical awareness, and they were able to design classroom lessons that integrated AI concepts into disciplinary instruction. Yet, the pattern of learning was significantly mediated by cultural and systemic contexts. The synthesis that follows articulates these patterns to show how AI literacy can function simultaneously as a universal pedagogical construct and as a culturally situated educational practice.

The analysis proceeds in five major stages. Firs we provide a synthesis of the learning outcomes across both cohorts, detailing the convergences and divergences in knowledge, ethics, and instructional design. Then we interpret the shared outcomes of the course as an intervention, identifying the course pedagogical features that transcended cultural boundaries. Next section examines the contextual and systemic factors that explain the observed cross-national divergence. Then we discuss the theoretical and practical implications for teacher preparation, curriculum design, and educational policy. Finally, we outline the study's primary contributions, acknowledges its limitations, and proposes directions for future research.

9.2 Synthesis of Empirical Findings

This section presents an integrated synthesis of the key empirical findings detailed in Chaps 6, 7, and 8. By aggregating the quantitative and qualitative data across the American and Chinese cohorts, we first establish the core learning outcomes of the intervention before moving to the contextual interpretation in subsequent sections. The analysis demonstrates that while the course successfully fostered measurable growth across all dimensions, the specific profiles of development were distinct across the national contexts.

9.2.1 *AI Content Knowledge Development*

As reported in Chap. 6, pre-service teachers in both cohorts demonstrated statistically significant improvement on the AI content knowledge test (U.S.: $M = 22.3 \rightarrow 31.7$, $d = 0.59$; China: $M = 20.8 \rightarrow 28.4$, $d = 0.47$; $p < .001$). These results confirm that the Five Big Ideas in AI framework is cognitively transferable across cultural contexts. A more granular analysis showed that the U.S. participants made their largest gains in Representation & Reasoning, an AI Big Idea emphasizing conceptual structures and systemic modeling, while their smallest growth was in the Learning Big Idea. The Chinese participants, by contrast, displayed stronger growth in Learning and Perception, Big Ideas closely tied to procedural and experiential exploration. Notably, the Chinese cohort exhibited their smallest gains in Societal Impact due to a ceiling effect from a high baseline score in that domain. These trends mirror broader educational orientations: the U.S. approach focusing on discussion-based pedagogy fostered conceptual abstraction, while China's structured inquiry promoting technical mastery. Both pathways resulted in comparable total knowledge gains but different cognitive profiles—a pattern that recurs throughout this synthesis.

9.2.2 *Ethical Awareness and Reasoning*

As detailed in Chap. 7, ethical awareness across FATES framework dimensions (Fairness, Accountability, Transparency, Environmental sustainability, and Societal impact) evolved significantly for all participants with both cohorts showing an overall mean increase (U.S. $\Delta M = 0.28$; China $\Delta M = 0.22$). Quantitatively, the U.S. cohort's most notable increase in concern was for the Environmental sustainability dimension ($\Delta M = 0.60$), shifting the focus to macro-level impact. Conversely, the Chinese cohort showed the largest internal shift in the Autonomy dimension ($\Delta M = 0.50$). Perceptions regarding Societal impact remained stable for both groups.

Qualitative data revealed three emergent trajectories: growth, disillusionment, and reluctance. These trajectories demonstrate how the emotional valence and focus of ethical concern differed. U.S. teachers often framed dilemmas in terms of personal responsibility, focusing on external governance (e.g., policy, legal liability, mandatory human-in-the-loop) and safety nets. Chinese teachers, however, invoked collective norms, focusing on systemic stability (e.g., educational adaptation, internal design efficiency, governmental accountability) and optimizing human capability within the prevailing technological narrative. This pattern aligns with cultural expectations of individual versus collective moral agency.

9.2.3 Instructional Design Practices

An analysis of lesson plans developed by pre-service teachers showed robust integration, with 73.8% of plans achieving Level 3 (interdisciplinary) or Level 4 (transdisciplinary) integration of AI literacy within discipline-specific content. This statistical stability confirms that the course fostered a shared pedagogical baseline and high capacity for deep AI literacy integration in both cohorts.

However, further thematic comparison revealed distinct strategic priorities in pedagogical goals, resulting in divergent instructional traditions:

- Chinese tradition (methodological mastery): Chinese participants demonstrated a significantly greater concentration on embedding AI as the core, active methodology for achieving disciplinary content mastery. Their strategic priority on problem framing (D1, 68.3%) and collaborative design (C2, 76.0%) confirms an instructional goal of achieving mastery through creation, with AI serving as the tool to codify, build, and verify the disciplinary concept.
- American tradition (critical oversight): American participants primarily used AI as a critical and ethical lens. Their strategic priority on digital agency (R2, 91.7%) and critical evaluation (D2, 86.7%) confirms an instructional goal of achieving critical oversight through governance, with AI serving as the lens to critique the societal impact of the discipline and formulate policy proposals.

In summary, the statistical stability in overall integration scores confirms a shared pedagogical baseline and high capacity for deep integration (Level 3/4) in both cohorts. This convergence of capacity coupled with the divergence in prioritized competencies (D1/C2 versus R2/D2) indicates that while both groups achieved high levels of AI literacy integration, they directed this shared capacity toward fundamentally different instructional goals.

9.2.4 Cross-Domain Patterns and Interdependencies

The analysis across the three domains, content knowledge, ethical reasoning, and instructional design practices, reveals a consistent and complex pattern: a convergence of capacity between the cohorts, coupled with a fundamental divergence in how that capacity is applied and interpreted. This divergence is systematically driven by two distinct, culturally mediated priorities: systemic governance and critical oversight (U.S.) and foundational mastery and solution-oriented design (China).

The primary pattern of convergence confirms the robust design of the curriculum and the transferability of AI literacy fundamentals. Both cohorts achieved comparable total knowledge gains despite different pacing, confirming that the Five Big Ideas in AI framework is cognitively transferable across institutional and cultural boundaries. Both cohorts demonstrated an overall increase in ethical awareness across the FATES dimensions. Both cohorts achieved a shared pedagogical baseline for integration, with 73.8% of lesson plans reaching Level 3 or 4 integration.

Where the cohorts diverged, the U.S. cohort revealed a consistent and coordinated set of priorities centered on systemic governance and critical oversight. The U.S. cohort's focus consistently centered on abstract systems, critical evaluation, and external regulation, framing AI literacy as a tool for oversight and personal responsibility. This was demonstrated through their largest cognitive gain in Representation & Reasoning, which equipped them with the necessary systems thinking to prioritize ethical concerns solvable by macro-level policy, such as the significant increase in concern for environmental sustainability. Consistent with this external focus, their shared pedagogical capacity was directed toward critical oversight, prioritizing competencies like digital agency and critical evaluation in their lesson plans. Overall, the U.S. cohort's cognitive strength in systemic modeling led them to prioritize ethical issues solvable by macro-level policy and to express this priority through instructional goals focused on critical evaluation and oversight.

Conversely, the Chinese cohort displayed an equally coordinated set of findings across all three domains, focusing consistently on foundational mastery and solution-oriented design as its core organizing principle. The Chinese cohort's focus consistently centered on procedural understanding, technical creation, and collective norms, framing AI literacy as a pathway to achieving social benefit and optimizing human capability. This was supported by their largest cognitive gains in Learning and Perception, the Big Ideas tied to procedural and experiential exploration, which translated directly into an instructional priority for methodological mastery (building and codifying concepts) using competencies like problem framing and collaborative design. Ethically, their largest concern shift was in autonomy, which aligned with a qualitative focus on internal design efficiency and systemic stability—optimizing the technology itself and maintaining human agency within the interface. Overall, the Chinese cohort's strong foundation in procedural knowledge translated directly into a pedagogical and ethical mandate for solution-oriented design and the stable optimization of human capability within the technological narrative.

9.3 Shared Learning Outcomes and Course Features

The synthesis of findings in Sect. 9.2 confirmed a shared baseline of success: statistically significant knowledge gains, moderate-to-strong growth in ethical awareness, and a high shared capacity for deep AI literacy integration in instructional design. These fundamental convergences suggest that the core design of the AI Literacy for Educators course possesses highly transferable pedagogical elements that successfully demonstrate consistency across distinct cultural and systemic educational contexts. This section interprets these shared outcomes, highlighting three features of the intervention—the conceptual framework, the systematic scaffolding, and the embedded ethical challenge—that emerged as consistently efficacious.

9.3.1 Efficacy of the Five Big Ideas in AI Framework

The Five Big Ideas in AI framework (Perception, Representation & Reasoning, Learning, Natural Interaction, and Societal Impact) proved to be a robust and adaptable cognitive tool. Its success rests on two features:

- Conceptual parsimony: The framework breaks down the complex field of AI into five distinct, yet interconnected, conceptual categories. This structured approach provided participants in both cohorts with a clear mental model, offering a crucial entry point for beginners, regardless of their disciplinary background or technological familiarity.
- Transferability to disciplinary contexts: By focusing on the underlying principles of computation (e.g., how machines learn or reason), rather than specific, rapidly changing technologies, the framework enabled preservice teachers to readily connect AI concepts to their respective subject areas. This facilitated the high integration capacity observed in Chap. 8, where teachers across disciplines could locate a relevant "Big Idea" to embed in their lesson plans.

9.3.2 Systematic Scaffolding for Pedagogical Application

The success of the intervention was driven by the coherent, phased structure within each Big Idea in AI module. This systematic approach moved participants from foundational conceptual learning to scaffolded pedagogical application, thereby creating an internal consistency between the content and the process of teacher preparation, which ultimately enabled the deep AI literacy integration.

- Foundational learning: Each module first provided instruction on the core Big Idea through the three-step process: Introduction → Inquiry-based exploration → Analysis of underlying principles. This sequence established the theoretical knowledge and critical ethical lens

- Iterative pedagogical scaffolding: The focus then shifted to pedagogical application. Participants analyzed the connections between AI concepts and core disciplinary practices using the Pedagogical Framework for AI Literacy. Crucially, they examined sample lessons integrating AI literacy into standards-based curricula across various grade bands (elementary, middle, and high school). This explicit modeling demonstrated how to integrate AI literacy not as an isolated topic but as an integral part of disciplinary learning.
- Culmination in DCR alignment: This full module sequence (Concept → Critique → Model → Design) acted as a direct, powerful learning model, which prepared participants for the design of their own lesson plans that integrated core concepts using the DCR cycle, making it easier for them to translate the instructional approach into the high-quality, deeply integrated lesson plans.

9.3.3 Ethical Reasoning as Embedded Practice

The course achieved universal ethical growth by mandating critical ethical analysis as an integral part of the three-step process for every Big Idea module. This structural mandate ensured that ethical discourse was not optional, but embedded into the learning process. By consistently challenging participants to analyze ethical implications and critically evaluate the potential and challenges of AI within the context of each Big Idea (e.g., the bias inherent in Perception or the accountability related to Reasoning), the course established a continuous habit of mind. This moved participants beyond basic awareness to a state of critical articulation, as demonstrated by the strong quantitative improvement in ethical reasoning scores.

9.3.4 Evidence of Shared Pedagogical Capacity

The ultimate indication of this cross-contextual efficacy is the shared high priority given to two AI literacy competencies in the lesson plans designed by the pre-service teachers: Prototyping and iterative testing (C1, ~ 98%) and critically evaluating AI applications (D2, ~ 91%). These high scores across both cohorts provide direct evidence that:

- The systematic instruction on the DCR model and the provision of sample lessons successfully established a high, shared technical capacity for prototyping (C1), enabling teachers to apply AI concepts in hands-on, constructive ways.
- The continuous ethical challenge embedded in every module successfully established the disposition for critical evaluation (D2), ensuring that critique and assessment of AI systems became an essential part of the instructional baseline for all participants.

In sum, the success of the intervention is attributable to a robust framework that provided structure, an internally consistent learning sequence that enforced application and reflection, and authentic content that guaranteed critical engagement. The next section shifts focus to the divergence in outcomes, analyzing the cultural and systemic factors that mediated this universal pedagogical success.

9.4 Cultural and Systemic Factors Shaping Divergent Outcomes

This section moves from describing the divergence to interpreting its cause, analyzing the specific cultural, educational, and systemic factors that mediated how AI literacy was received, prioritized, and ultimately enacted by the pre-service teachers from the United States and China.

9.4.1 Cultural Framing of Moral Agency and Responsibility

The most profound divergence lies in the framing of ethical awareness and responsibility, which appears to align with distinct societal narratives U.S. participants personalized ethical dilemmas regarding the self, society, and technology. The dominant disillusionment trajectory in the U.S. cohort highlights a cultural orientation toward individual responsibility and skepticism toward large systems. U.S. participants frequently personalized ethical dilemmas ("How can I ensure fairness?"), a pattern that may contribute to moral fatigue and heightened concern when confronted with systemic bias. Conversely, the high rate of the growth trajectory in the Chinese cohort resonates with broader cultural frameworks prioritizing collective agency and policy-driven solutions. Chinese participants framed ethical issues within established societal norms or national goals ("How can schools ensure AI supports moral cultivation?"), viewing ethical problems as collective challenges to be managed through systemic design and technological advancement, rather than individual oversight. These ethical framings were reinforced by varying national narratives around technology.

While these patterns are distinct in our sample, they should be interpreted as context-dependent trends rather than absolute cultural determinants, as individual variation existed within both cohorts.

9.4.2 *Divergent Educational Traditions and Instructional Goals*

The patterns observed in lesson plan design were not random, but rather a robust reflection of established national pedagogical traditions and their definitions of educational success. Both cohorts demonstrated a high capacity for deep integration, but they applied this capacity to fundamentally different instructional goals:

- The American critical oversight tradition: This tradition reflects U.S. educational values emphasizing critical thinking, student voice, and socio-political critique. The American cohort showed a significantly higher priority for digital agency (R2, 91.7%), coupled with a high focus on critical evaluation (D2, 86.7%). This solidifies the instructional goal of achieving critical oversight through governance, where AI serves as an ethical and critical lens to formulate policy principles and challenge power structures, often leveraging the Reflect component to challenge the discipline itself (e.g., policy-making in social studies).
- The Chinese methodological mastery tradition: This tradition aligns with the value placed on rigorous technical application, cooperative work, and demonstration of disciplinary mastery. The Chinese cohort placed a significantly higher priority on problem framing (D1, 68.3%) and collaborative design (C2, 76.0%). This confirms their instructional goal: to achieve indispensable mastery through creation, using AI as the active methodological tool to codify, build, and verify the disciplinary concept through complex, multi-step, and collaborative functional prototyping.

9.5 Implications for Teacher Preparation, Curriculum Design, and Educational Policy

The findings of this cross-national study yield clear implications for advancing artificial intelligence (AI) literacy within teacher education. Across both national contexts (the United States and China), the results affirm that AI literacy is best positioned as a pedagogical foundation rather than a technological enrichment (Gu & Ericson, 2025; Zhou et al., 2020). The AI Literacy for Educators course successfully achieved this transformation by structuring the intervention around three key, universally effective design features: the cognitive coherence of the Five Big Ideas in AI framework, systematic scaffolding for practical application, and mandatory integration of critical ethical analysis. This pedagogical model equipped educators with the conceptual fluency, ethical awareness, and instructional adaptability required to prepare students for an intelligent age.

The core structure enabling the application and sustained practice of this learning is the Pedagogical Framework for AI Literacy, which services as an exemplar model that successfully integrates AI content knowledge (Five Big Ideas in AI), instructional process (Human-Centered Design), and learner development principles (Science of Learning and Development) for use in instructional design. Translating this framework from theory into practice requires attention to three interrelated domains: the adaptation of the framework to diverse contexts, the strengthening of teacher-preparation programs, and the development of coherent policy support.

9.5.1 Adapting the Pedagogical Framework for Diverse Contexts

Adapting the Pedagogical Framework for AI Literacy for different cultural and systemic settings is essential for ensuring its scalability and relevance. While the framework's tripartite structure is conceptually universal, its ethical and developmental dimensions could benefit from careful recalibration to reflect local pedagogical traditions and societal values.

The ethical component of the framework—which encourages a continuous critical habit of mind—is best approached through the local lens of moral agency. In collectivist educational cultures such as China's, for instance, the curriculum might prioritize harmony, civic duty, and moral cultivation, linking AI use to collective well-being (reflecting the growth trajectory). In the United States, by contrast, the same ethical dimension is encouraged to foreground student agency, equity, and critical inquiry, prompting learners to question algorithmic authority and design for inclusion (aligning with the critical oversight tradition). Contextual exemplars—drawn from local issues such as data privacy in U.S. schools or AI-enabled national examinations in China—can help teachers anchor global concepts within familiar realities.

Adaptation also extends to the practical elements of the instructional process, particularly assessment and technology integration. Existing assessment tools can be productively reinterpreted to accommodate differing rhetorical and evaluative norms: concise ethical statements may demonstrate depth in exam-oriented cultures, whereas extended reflective writing may better capture reasoning in discussion-based systems. Finally, the framework remains flexible regarding technological infrastructure. Both high-tech and unplugged pathways can support the same learning goals, whether through digital simulations or low-resource analog tasks that visualize algorithmic reasoning. Such adaptability confirms the framework's value as a globally coherent yet locally meaningful model.

9.5.2 Strengthening Teacher-Preparation Programs

Embedding AI literacy within teacher education requires a structural and pedagogical reconfiguration of how teachers are prepared to teach emerging technologies. The evidence from both sites suggests that AI literacy could be conceptualized as a developmental strand extending across the entirety of preservice training. Foundational coursework could be structured to introduce the AI content knowledge alongside FATES principles (Fairness, Accountability, Transparency, Environmental sustainability, and Societal impact). Subsequent methods courses might prioritize focus on lesson design for AI literacy integration, allowing preservice teachers to effectively apply the principles underlying the Pedagogical Framework for AI Literacy in their K-12 content areas during field-based practicum experiences. This vertical alignment enables a developmental progression from conceptual comprehension to pedagogical enactment that maps onto the Framework's architecture.

Teacher educators are encouraged to explicitly model the teaching of AI literacy (teaching about AI) by demonstrating how to integrate the DCR cycle into their own university coursework using both high-tech and unplugged activities. Furthermore, when instructors apply AI-supported tools (teaching with AI), they could simultaneously model how to critically evaluate the pedagogical and ethical implications of those technologies firsthand for their future classrooms.

Developing teachers' professional dispositions toward AI—particularly ethical reflection and civic responsibility—is a third essential element. Structured reflection protocols could be implemented to encourage preservice teachers to interrogate their own assumptions about algorithmic fairness and data use in schooling (Su & Zhong, 2022), thereby strengthening their moral reasoning and aligning professional identity with responsible innovation.

9.5.3 Coherent Policy Support

The findings suggest that system-level support is critical to ensure the effective adoption and sustained quality of AI literacy instruction across teacher preparation and K-12 schools. Teacher-education institutions could benefit from viewing AI literacy as a baseline competence within professional standards rather than an optional enrichment. National authorities could then define measurable outcomes that position AI literacy as a component of pedagogical expertise rather than technical specialization (Zhou et al., 2020). These outcomes might map onto domains such as instructional planning, ethical reasoning, formative assessment, and learner support. Policy instruments can then direct funding toward curriculum development, translation of open educational resources, and large-scale faculty-training initiatives that build institutional capacity to prepare preservice teachers to apply the core principles of the Pedagogical Framework for AI Literacy in K-12 settings.

Crucially, expanding this support to the in-service workforce requires acknowledging that active practitioners face distinct constraints compared to preservice teachers. Unlike university students, in-service teachers operate under significant time pressures, rigid curricular mandates, and often fragmented professional development opportunities. Therefore, for the framework to be scalable beyond teacher preparation programs, policy support must go beyond one-off workshops. It requires systemic coordination—such as job-embedded coaching, micro-credentials, and administrative provisions for planning time—that empowers teachers to adapt the DCR cycle within their existing constraints. Without this structural support, even a robust pedagogical framework risks being viewed as an additive burden rather than a transformative tool.

Equity and inclusion should remain the guiding ethos of these policies. Governments and accrediting bodies should guarantee that AI-literacy resources, including those supporting both high-tech and unplugged learning (Sect. 9.5.1), are available across linguistic, cultural, and socioeconomic boundaries. Ethical governance should be embedded in all teacher-education policies through mandatory coursework on responsible AI, data privacy, and digital citizenship (Owoc et al., 2021). Cross-sector collaboration between universities, K–12 systems, and technology developers could also be formalized through policy incentives, ensuring partnerships are guided by human-centered principles of responsible innovation.

9.6 Conclusions

This comparative study (Chaps. 5, 6, 7, and 8) makes several significant contributions to the growing field of AI literacy in teacher education:

- This work provides initial cross-national evidence (U.S. and China) suggesting that the unified structure of AI content knowledge (Five Big Ideas in AI) combined with the DCR cycle is an effective and transferable model for increasing teacher competency. The shared outcomes (knowledge gains and high integration capacity) empirically support the model's structural integrity against diverse cultural filters.
- The study moves beyond viewing AI literacy as a singular technical skill set by suggesting its culturally mediated nature. The observed divergence in ethical framing (individual vs. collective moral agency) and instructional goals (critical oversight vs. methodological mastery) indicates that the enactment of AI literacy is inextricably linked to national pedagogical traditions and socio-political values.
- By synthesizing data across knowledge, ethics, and practice, the study suggests key cross-domain relationships. Specifically, it supports the hypothesis that mandatory ethical critique functions as a cognitive catalyst for conceptual mastery (ethics-as-catalyst) and that ethical insight serves as a motivational bridge for pedagogical innovation (ethical-to-practice transfer).

The interpretation of these findings should be viewed in light of several methodological limitations associated with the design of the course intervention. The study utilized a quasi-experimental pre/post-test design across two intact, geographically separated cohorts. This approach, while necessary for the ecological validity of the study, prevents definitive causal claims about the intervention and limits the ability to control for all pre-existing cultural or systemic differences between the two national contexts. The findings are limited to the immediate efficacy of a single, concentrated course intervention. They do not account for the long-term retention of knowledge and skills or the systemic factors involved in scaling the intervention across institutions. While the lesson plans provided a robust measure of instructional design capacity, they are not a direct measure of teaching enactment or student learning outcomes. The study cannot account for how the preservice teachers' lesson plans would perform in live K-12 classrooms. efficacy of a single, concentrated course intervention. They do not account for the long-term retention of knowledge and skills or the systemic factors involved in scaling the intervention across institutions.

To address the limitation of analyzing instructional intent versus reality, future research must expand its methodological scope beyond document analysis. Empirical studies utilizing classroom observations and fidelity of implementation protocols are necessary to determine if the high-quality integration observed in lesson plans translates into effective pedagogical enactment. Such studies should investigate how preservice teachers navigate real-time classroom constraints, such as student misconceptions or technical failures, when integrating the AI literacy integrated lessons they designed.

Based on these limitations and the findings regarding cross-national divergence, we proposed the following avenues for future research:

- Future research could track participants from the American and Chinese cohorts into their first 1–3 years of professional practice. A longitudinal design is necessary to assess the persistence of the observed ethical dispositions (growth, disillusionment, reluctance trajectories) and how the prioritized AI literacy competencies (R2 vs. D1/C2) actually manifest under the institutional constraints of their respective school systems.
- To further explore the global adaptability and local responsiveness of the Pedagogical Framework for AI Literacy, future research should extend the study to different educational systems (e.g., Europe, Latin America). Such expansion would deepen the understanding of how educational values in varying cultural settings mediate the translation of a globally adaptable AI literacy model into specific pedagogical traditions.

To summarize, the implications of this study converge on a single imperative: AI literacy should be institutionalized as a foundational dimension of teacher education, centered on pedagogy rather than technical specialization. The success of the intervention described in this book confirms that this shift is feasible. The Pedagogical Framework for AI Literacy provides a proven, effective instructional design model for teachers to realize this transformation in K-12 settings. When the principles derived from the course's success are adapted responsively to local contexts, embedded vertically across preservice and in-service learning, and supported by coherent policy structures, the framework can prepare educators worldwide to lead students in engaging with AI critically, ethically, and creatively. Such integration redefines teacher education for the intelligent age—linking global aspirations for innovation with the enduring humanistic mission of schooling.

References

Gu, X., & Ericson, B. J. (2025). AI literacy in K-12 and higher education in the wake of generative AI: An integrative review. In L. Porter, N. Brown, B. Morrison, & C.S. Montero (Eds.) *Proceedings of the 2025 ACM conference on international computing education research* (Vol. 1, pp. 125–140). Association for Computing Machinery. https://doi.org/10.1145/3702652.3744217

Owoc, M. L., Sawicka, A., & Weichbroth, P. (2021). Artificial intelligence technologies in education: Benefits, challenges and strategies of implementation. In M.L. Owoc, & M. Pondel (Eds.), *Artificial Intelligence for knowledge management. AI4KM 2019.* (vol. 599, pp. 37–58). IFIP Advances in Information and Communication Technology, Springer. https://doi.org/10.1007/978-3-030-85001-2_4

Su, J., & Zhong, Y. (2022). Artificial intelligence (AI) in early childhood education: Curriculum design and future directions. *Computers and Education: Artificial Intelligence, 3*, Article 100072. https://doi.org/10.1016/j.caeai.2022.100072

Zhou, X., Van Brummelen, J., & Lin, P. (2020). *Designing AI learning experiences for K-12: Emerging works, future opportunities and a design framework.* (arXiv:2009.10228). arXiv. https://doi.org/10.48550/arXiv.2009.10228

Epilogue: Reflections, Recommendations, and Future Research

This book has detailed the urgent need for a unified approach to AI literacy in K–12 education, presenting a comprehensive pedagogical framework validated through cross-cultural research. As we reach the conclusion of this study, we offer these final reflections and strategic recommendations, recognizing that the road to truly inclusive and effective AI education is just beginning.

Revisiting the Book's Core Contributions

This book has advanced a unified and multidimensional vision of AI literacy grounded in conceptual understanding, ethical reasoning, learner agency, and responsible application. It argues that preparing teachers and students for an AI-driven world requires far more than technological familiarity; it calls for a redefinition of what it means to learn, teach, and act in the age of intelligent systems. The proposed *Pedagogical Framework for AI Literacy* provides this foundation. Anchored in the Five Big Ideas in AI as the content dimension, Human-Centered Design (HCD) as the process dimension, and the Science of Learning and Development (SoLD) as the dispositional dimension, the framework offers a theoretically robust yet practically adaptable structure for integrating AI literacy into diverse educational settings.

Central to this framework is the Design–Create–Reflect (DCR) cycle, which operationalizes AI literacy into implementable instructional and assessment practices. By guiding educators to design authentic learning experiences, create tangible solutions, and reflect critically on ethical and social implications, the DCR cycle transforms AI literacy from abstract concept to actionable pedagogy. Through the cross-national case studies conducted in the United States and China, the framework's effectiveness was tested across distinct educational systems and cultural contexts. The results demonstrate its flexibility in supporting varied learning goals, curricular designs, and educator needs. The integration of empirical research, lesson-planning tools, and

I. Lyublinskaya and X. Du, *A Pedagogical Framework for K–12 AI Literacy*, Springer Texts in Education, https://doi.org/10.1007/978-3-032-23570-1

teacher narratives throughout the book illustrates how AI literacy can move from theory to classroom reality—demonstrating that structured scaffolds and reflective models effectively prepare preservice teachers to integrate complex AI concepts and ethical discussions into their future practice.

Practical Recommendations for Stakeholders

The findings presented in this book have important implications for educators, curriculum designers, and education leaders who are working to advance AI literacy at scale. For educators, the DCR cycle offers a practical method for planning lessons that promote technical understanding, ethical reflection, and student-driven inquiry. To maximize reach and relevance, teachers must shift toward a cross-disciplinary approach, deliberately integrating AI literacy into existing curricula across all subject areas, from analyzing algorithmic bias in civics class to exploring GenAI in a creative writing context. Teachers are encouraged to adopt hands-on, interdisciplinary projects that connect AI to real-world challenges, student identities, and community issues, ensuring that learning remains both relevant and equitable. Ethical reasoning should be introduced early and woven throughout instruction, using classroom dilemmas, peer discussions, and collaboratively developed norms to help students navigate questions of fairness, privacy, and accountability.

For curriculum developers, adopting the Five Big Ideas in AI as the core content structure for AI literacy materials can ensure conceptual consistency while allowing flexibility across grade levels and subject areas. Curricular materials and resources should be designed to support critical reflection, civic engagement, and the use of culturally relevant examples that reflect the diversity of learners and societies affected by AI. Developing adaptable templates, annotated exemplars, and open-ended projects can further support teachers in embedding AI literacy within existing disciplinary standards without overburdening instructional time.

For policymakers and education leaders, the evidence underscores the need for systemic change. At this level, the incorporation of AI literacy is necessary within digital literacy standards, 21st-century skills frameworks, and teacher certification pathways. To support this mandate, effective professional learning programs are essential for integrating ethics, design thinking, and interdisciplinary teaching strategies to foster both educators' technical competence and their instructional efficacy. Furthermore, this system requires a foundation of equitable infrastructure, such as reliable access to AI tools, open-source development environments, and culturally inclusive curricula, to ensure that all schools and communities can participate meaningfully in the AI transformation. These investments are not merely technical; they are civic commitments to fairness, opportunity, and human flourishing in a rapidly automated world.

Future Research Directions

While the studies presented in this book validate the utility and early efficacy of the Pedagogical Framework for AI Literacy, they also highlight critical areas for further investigation that will help shape the next generation of inquiry. Future studies should examine the longitudinal impacts of AI literacy education—how teachers and students sustain, transfer, and evolve their knowledge, ethical awareness, and civic engagement over time. Importantly, there is a growing need to develop validated assessment instruments that measure AI literacy across cognitive, ethical, and creative dimensions. The scope of research must widen to include rigorous implementation studies. We call for mixed-methods investigations that link teacher preparation directly to K–12 student outcomes, assessing whether the teacher's mastery of the DCR cycle results in measurable gains in their students' technical fluency and ethical reasoning. These assessments must move beyond self-reported understanding, requiring performance-based methods that capture both process and reflection, and allowing researchers to observe how learners operationalize ethical reasoning and agency to negotiate real dilemmas of data use, fairness, and algorithmic bias in AI-rich learning environments.

Cross-cultural and disciplinary adaptation remains another critical area of focus, as educators continue to localize and personalize AI literacy frameworks to reflect diverse epistemologies, languages, and value systems. Furthermore, exploring this adaptation necessitates a deeper look into the relationship between AI literacy, equity, and identity formation, especially for historically marginalized learners whose experiences with algorithmic systems are often shaped by structural inequities. Finally, researchers should expand research–practice partnerships that co-design and evaluate scalable, justice-centered interdisciplinary models for AI literacy integration—initiatives that unite teachers, technologists, and communities in the shared pursuit of ethical innovation.

Concluding Reflections

AI literacy is no longer a peripheral topic; we believe it is a foundational competency for living, learning, and participating in a society shaped by intelligent technologies. The frameworks and studies presented in this book provide a roadmap for how schools, teacher preparation programs, and policymakers can build meaningful, ethical, and inclusive AI learning environments. Yet this roadmap is only the beginning. The future of AI literacy depends on continued collaboration—between researchers who refine models, educators who implement and adapt them, and leaders who enable conditions for equity and innovation.

At its core, our work affirms that AI literacy is not about replacing human intelligence but enriching it. We maintain that it is about equipping every learner with the understanding, ethical grounding, and creative confidence to engage with AI as both a tool and a topic of inquiry. As algorithms become woven into the fabric of everyday life, the central question for education shifts from *What can AI do?* to *What should humans do with AI—and for one another?*

This book ends, therefore, with our personal invitation to you: to co-create a future where all learners—regardless of geography, culture, or background—are empowered to understand, critique, and shape the AI systems that shape their world. It is in this shared endeavor that we place our hope, as it lies the enduring promise of education: to build not only intelligent technologies, but a more intelligent, ethical, and compassionate humanity.

The Authors

Glossary

Algorithmic bias (fairness/bias): A systematic error in a computer system, typically arising from skewed training data or flawed assumptions, that produces prejudicial outcomes which discriminate against specific groups and amplify existing societal inequities.

Artificial Intelligence (AI) literacy: A multidimensional competency necessary for future-ready citizenship that balances foundational technical knowledge (**Understand**), critical reasoning (**Evaluate**), and responsible application (**Use**) of AI technologies.

Autonomy/Privacy: An ethical dimension encompassing the fundamental right to privacy, the protection of personal data, and an individual's ability to maintain control, self-determination, and freedom of choice in an increasingly automated world.

Base rate problem: A statistical issue where reliability measures (like Cohen's Kappa) become biased and fail to accurately reflect true consensus between raters because the categorical data is heavily imbalanced or one score is highly prevalent.

Cohen's *d* (effect size): A statistical measure used to demonstrate the practical significance and magnitude of an observed change (such as learning gains or shifts in ethical perceptions), which is particularly critical for interpreting results when small sample sizes limit the statistical significance of *p*-values

Confirmatory Factor Analysis (CFA): A structural equation modeling technique used to empirically test construct validity by explicitly comparing a hypothesized theoretical structure against alternative parsimonious models

Construct validity: The extent to which an assessment tool accurately captures the specific theoretical concept it was designed to evaluate.

Constructivism: A foundational learning theory positing that individuals actively construct their own understanding and knowledge of the world through experiences, social interactions, and reflection, rather than passively receiving information.

Content validity: The extent to which an instrument or framework comprehensively and accurately measures the specific domain it is designed to measure.

I. Lyublinskaya and X. Du, *A Pedagogical Framework for K–12 AI Literacy*, Springer Texts in Education, https://doi.org/10.1007/978-3-032-23570-1

Design-Create-Reflect (DCR) Cycle: The core pedagogical cycle of the **Pedagogical Framework for AI Literacy** that operationalizes AI learning. It guides teachers and students through iterative **Design** (empathetic inquiry and problem framing), **Create** (prototyping and collaborative testing), and **Reflect** (metacognitive and ethical self-assessment) components.

Digital agency: An individual's capacity to act independently, make intentional choices, and exert meaningful control over their digital footprint and interactions within complex algorithmic systems.

Disciplinary integration: A pedagogical continuum of knowledge synthesis that progresses from a strictly single-subject focus (**intradisciplinary**) and additive side-by-side approaches (**multidisciplinary**), to true methodological fusion (**interdisciplinary**) and completely holistic, boundary-transcending frameworks (**transdisciplinary**).

Environmental sustainability: The responsible management and conservation of natural resources and ecosystems to fulfill current societal and economic needs without compromising the ability of future generations to meet their own.

Evaluate (AI literacy domain): A core domain of AI literacy centering on an individual's capacity to critically assess the ethical, civic, and societal implications of AI technologies, such as algorithmic bias, privacy, and systemic inequalities.

FATES Framework: An expanded ethical AI framework comprising five core dimensions: Fairness/Bias, Autonomy/Privacy, Transparency/Explainability, Environmental Sustainability, and Societal Impact.

Five Big Ideas in AI: A foundational framework that defines K-12 AI content knowledge across five big ideas: Perception, Representation & Reasoning, Learning, Natural Interaction, and Societal Impact.

Future-ready citizenship: The possession of adaptive competencies —specifically critical thinking, digital agency, and complex problem-solving —that equip individuals to navigate, reconcile tensions, and take responsibility in evolving sociotechnical contexts.

Generative AI (GenAI): Artificial intelligence systems capable of generating novel text, images, and code by synthesizing complex patterns from massive training datasets; while they offer valuable step-by-step problem-solving support, they require explicit human judgment to mitigate the risks of cognitive offloading and deskilling.

Human-Centered Design (HCD): A problem-solving framework and development approach that prioritizes the needs, contexts, and behaviors of users, ensuring that technological systems are built to actively support human agency and well-being rather than forcing individuals to adapt to the technology.

Interdisciplinary: A fusion-based approach that actively synthesizes methodologies, perspectives, and concepts from two or more distinct academic fields to create a new, integrated understanding of a complex issue.

Inter-rater reliability: The degree of consistency and agreement between independent coders applying a scoring protocol.

Intradisciplinary: An approach to learning or problem-solving that remains completely confined within the boundaries of a single academic discipline, focusing strictly on the internal connections between its specific subfields.

Learning (AI Big Idea): A core concept in AI encompassing the principles of machine learning—including supervised, unsupervised, and reinforcement learning—and exploring how algorithms iteratively improve their performance through exposure to data.

Mixed Methods Design: A research approach used to study complex phenomena by intentionally integrating quantitative data and qualitative data to provide a more comprehensive understanding than either method could achieve alone.

Multidisciplinary: An additive educational approach where a complex theme or problem is examined through the distinct lenses of multiple academic disciplines, bringing subjects together side-by-side without merging their core methodologies.

Multivariate Analysis of Covariance (MANCOVA): A statistical technique used to test for significant differences between group means across multiple dependent variables simultaneously, while mathematically controlling for the effects of one or more continuous covariates (such as pre-test scores or baseline demographics) that might otherwise skew the results.

Multivariate Analysis of Variance (MANOVA): A statistical procedure used to test for significant differences between independent groups across two or more dependent variables simultaneously, allowing researchers to account for the correlations between related outcomes while reducing the risk of statistical error.

Natural Interaction (AI Big Idea): A core idea in AI exploring how AI systems communicate and collaborate with humans through natural language processing, voice/gesture recognition, and multimodal interfaces.

Parallel Analysis (PA): A data-driven statistical test used to determine the empirical dimensionality of a framework by comparing the eigenvalues from actual data, which represent the amount of variance explained by each potential factor, against the eigenvalues derived from randomly generated datasets.

Pedagogical Framework for AI Literacy: A research-informed instructional framework structured around three interconnected pillars: AI content knowledge based on the Five Big Ideas, instructional processes guided by Human-Centered Design, and learner development rooted in the Science of Learning and Development principles

Perception (AI Big Idea): A core idea in AI addressing how automated systems sense, capture, and interpret data from the physical world through modalities such as computer vision, sound, and touch.

Quasi-experimental design: A research methodology used to evaluate the causal impact of an intervention without the use of random assignment, relying instead on pre-existing groups (such as intact classrooms) or natural variations in exposure to the treatment.

Representation & Reasoning (AI Big Idea): A core idea in AI addressing how automated systems encode knowledge (representation) and perform logical inference (reasoning) to bridge data and action.

SAMR: A pedagogical framework (Substitution, Augmentation, Modification, and Redefinition) used to evaluate the degree of technology integration in educational settings, illustrating a progression from the simple digital replacement of traditional tools to the creation of entirely new, previously inconceivable learning tasks

Science of Learning and Development (SoLD): An interdisciplinary framework synthesizing research from neuroscience and developmental psychology to demonstrate that human cognition and learning are deeply shaped by social contexts, emotional states, and cultural identities.

Scree plot: A line graph of eigenvalues—representing the variance explained by each factor—used to visually estimate the number of latent variables in a dataset, which is often evaluated alongside more rigorous, data-driven methods to confirm a framework's true dimensionality.

Societal Impact (AI Big Idea & FATES Dimension): A dual-purpose concept serving both as a foundational AI Big Idea—introducing the broader ethical dilemmas and unintended consequences of intelligent systems—and as a core dimension of the FATES framework, which critically examines AI's profound socioeconomic impacts, such as job displacement and civic disruption

Transdisciplinary: A highly integrated conceptual framework that transcends traditional academic silos entirely, synthesizing knowledge from multiple disciplines alongside real-world stakeholder perspectives to solve complex, unstructured sociotechnical problems.

Transparency/Explainability: An ethical dimension within the FATES framework requiring that AI systems' functions, decisions, and limitations are clear, auditable, and comprehensible to users, which is essential to mitigate the "black box" problem and build public trust.

Triangulation: A mixed-methods research strategy that cross-validates findings by integrating distinct data sources—such as quantitative metrics and qualitative themes—to ensure both the reliability and the contextual depth of the final conclusions.

Understand (AI literacy domain): A domain of AI literacy centering on an individual's foundational understanding of what AI is, how it operates, and the core structures behind AI systems, such as algorithms and feedback loops.

Understanding by Design (UbD): An educational planning framework that utilizes a "backward design" approach, requiring educators to first identify the desired learning outcomes, then determine acceptable evidence of learning, and finally plan the instructional activities to achieve those goals.

Use (AI literacy domain): A domain of AI literacy referring to an individual's capacity to meaningfully apply, design, iterate on, and reflect upon AI technologies in contextually relevant, responsible, and ethically informed ways.

Index

I. Lyublinskaya and X. Du, *A Pedagogical Framework for K–12 AI Literacy*, Springer Texts in Education, https://doi.org/10.1007/978-3-032-23570-1

The manufacturer's authorised representative in the EU is Springer Nature Customer Service Centre GmbH, Europaplatz 3, 69115 Heidelberg, Germany. If you have any concerns regarding our products, please contact ProductSafety@springernature.com

Printed and bound by CPI Group (UK) Ltd, Croydon, CR0 4YY
12/10/2026
02231745-0001